Berlitz®

Costa del Sol
& Andalucía

Text by Norman Renouf
Updated by Pam Barrett
Edited by Jeffery Pike
Managing Editor: Tony Halliday

D1742590

Berlitz® POCKET GUIDE

Costa del Sol
& Andalucía

Twelfth Edition 2004 (Reprinted 2004)

PHOTOGRAPHY

AGE Fotostock 23; Chris Coe 19, 24, 26, 29, 30, 33, 34, 39, 42, 55, 56, 59, 63, 64, 71, 98, 99; Jerry Dennis 6, 8, 9, 14, 16, 32, 37, 40, 41, 45, 47, 48, 49, 51, 52, 61, 62, 68, 77, 78, 81, 84, 87, 89, 92, 95, 101, 102; Mark Read 11, 13, 17, 18, 21, 35, 44, 46, 57, 58, 66, 67, 72, 74, 78, 79, 82, 85, 88, 91, 96; Real Escula Andaluza del Arte Ecuestre 60
Cover: Chris Coe

CONTACTING THE EDITORS

Every effort has been made to provide accurate information in this publication, but changes are inevitable. The publisher cannot be responsible for any resulting loss, inconvenience or injury. We would appreciate it if readers would call our attention to any errors or outdated information by contacting Berlitz Publishing, PO Box 7910, London SE1 1WE, England. Fax: (44) 20 7403 0290;
e-mail: berlitz@apaguide.co.uk
www.berlitzpublishing.com

The magnificent Mezquita in Córdoba was once the largest mosque in the western Islamic world (see page 66)

Puerto Banús is the glitzy resort favoured by the international jet set (see page 39)

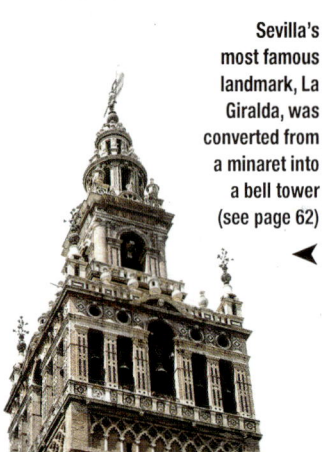

Sevilla's most famous landmark, La Giralda, was converted from a minaret into a bell tower (see page 62)

TOP TEN ATTRACTIONS

Ronda's ancient bullring is the birthplace of the modern bullfight (see page 53)

The mighty Alcazaba looms over the town of Almería (see page 52)

Granada was the capital of the Moorish Nasrid dynasty, who celebrated their power by building the sublime hilltop palace, the Alhambra (see page 72)

The Costa del Sol is blessed with many miles of sandy beaches

Jerez de la Frontera, the heart of Spanish horsemanship and the home of sherry (see page 58)

The Cueva de Nerja, a huge limestone cavern (see page 49)

Gibraltar is an unmistakably British enclave on the Spanish coast (see page 42)

CONTENTS

A ➤ in the text denotes a highly recommended sight

THE REGION AND ITS PEOPLE

For thousands of years, the people of the Costa del Sol, except when invaded or in times of war, went about their business oblivious to the concerns of the outside world. But in the last half of the 20th century that changed dramatically when the Costa transformed itself from a collection of sleepy towns and fishing villages into the playground of the Western world.

Strung along the southern coast of Spain between Gibraltar in the southwest and Almería to the east, this Mediterranean coastline encompasses parts of Cádiz, Málaga, Granada and Almería – four of the eight provinces of Andalucía, Spain's southernmost autonomous community. The other provinces are Huelva, adjoining Portugal and the Atlantic Ocean, and landlocked Sevilla, Córdoba and Jaén. Surprisingly, the beaches on the Costa del Sol are not wide, with miles of yellow sand, as on the Atlantic coast. Rather, never far from the mountains and in some sections directly next to them, they are usually composed of a dull grey sand that has been formed by the erosion of these same mountains. In fact, many of the beaches aren't particularly attractive, often paralleling the busy E15/N340 highway that runs the length of the Costa del Sol. And in summer, some of them can be more than a little crowded.

So what attracts millions of visitors from numerous countries every year? Well, for a start, bountiful sunshine almost all year round: the Costa del Sol has an average of 320 cloud-free days a year. Because the region is protected by an almost endless wall of mountains – the Sierra Nevada to the east of Málaga and the Serranía de Ronda to the west – it is

The Alcaicería in Granada, once the silk market of the Moors

spared the harsh, arid heat of the inland plateau. Temperatures in the summer rarely rise above 30°C (86°F). In addition, such a climate encourages an easygoing atmosphere; local people, despite having had their way of life changed dramatically, still retain a gregarious, garrulous and generous nature, and tourists are made to feel very welcome here.

West to Tarifa

Málaga's international airport is the primary gateway to the Costa del Sol, which can be subdivided into two sections, west and east of Málaga. The more familiar image of the Costa del Sol is to be found to the west, where development reaches far back from the beaches. In the original tourist boom town of Torremolinos, high-rise hotels and squat apartment blocks loom above the waterfront promenade and the bustling back streets are lined with pubs, clubs,

Málaga's Plaza de la Constitución

discos, chip shops, curry houses and other amenities familiar to British tourists. The apartment complexes around the marina at Benalmádena, however, are far more attractive than the unregulated sprawl found in its near-neighbour, and show what can be achieved with a little foresight.

Marbella, though, is very different. The original playground of the 1960s jet set and the upmarket showcase of the Costa del Sol, it was

Puerto Banús

first put on the map by Prince Alfonso von Hohenlohe in the 1950s. Today, movie stars, oil-rich Arab potentates and other celebrities keep it in the news. In more recent years, though, neighbouring Puerto Banús has emerged as the place to be seen. Huge and magnificent yachts are moored in the marina, gourmet restaurants line the harbour, and sophisticated stores abound. Towards Estepona, hotels and apartment complexes diminish in number, but are no less stylish, as stretches of empty beach and green hillsides claim the landscape.

Continuing on, the familiar silhouette of the Rock of Gibraltar dominates the skyline. Should you want to investigate further, it is accessible by the road that leads off the E15/N340 at San Roque and ends at La Linea de la Concepción, the border with Gibraltar. Across the bay, Algeciras is the gateway to North Africa, which can be seen, though often through a haze, just across the Strait of Gibraltar. There are even better views from the *mirador* (viewpoint) on the hill as the road winds around to Tarifa, the western end of the Costa del Sol.

East to Almería

The eastern part of the Costa, from Málaga to Almería, is quieter and less intensively developed. Rincón de la Victoria and Torrox are the first couple of resorts, but you will have to travel to Nerja, the largest resort on this stretch of coast, to find anything approaching those in the western section. Even here, the ambience is considerably quieter. Very soon, after the mountains begin to drop precipitously towards the sea, wonderful views can be had from the road, with family resorts like La Herradura and Almuñécar nestled in bays.

This stretch of the Costa del Sol, in the Provincia de Granada, is now known as the Costa Tropical. Motril sits in the middle of an unexpectedly lush green delta planted variously with avocados, citrus fruits, sugar cane, bananas and bamboo, and is guarded to the west by Salobreña and its Moorish castle. Motril to Adra is a conservation area; besides being by far the least built-up of any area on the whole Costa del Sol, it is scenically the most dramatic. Conversely, the route across the plain after leaving Adra is the dreariest along the whole coast. Fortunately, the mountains again meet the sea close to the town of Aguadulce, enlivening the last few kilometres into the city of Almería.

Andalucía's Attractions

The attributes that led to the initial development of the Costa del Sol remain its major attractions. Air travel to the Costa is inexpensive and easy, with a wide choice of scheduled and charter flights. It has good beaches and the sun can be relied upon to shine nine days out of 10. It is one of the liveliest and most cosmopolitan resort areas in the world, and there is an extensive array of attractions that would be difficult to find in such close proximity elsewhere. Skiing in the sierras, then nipping down to the coast for a swim and a drink is just one of them.

Andalucían landscape at Antequera, a typical *pueblo blanco* in the mountains north of Málaga

Visitors who investigate beyond the beaches will find a collection of picturesque whitewashed villages. Beyond the mountains are numerous ancient towns whose histories are known throughout the world. There's Sevilla, famed for its bullfights and flamenco; Córdoba, the first capital of Moorish Spain; and Granada, capital of the last Moorish kingdom on the Iberian peninsula and home of the magnificent Alhambra palace. This is also where you'll find Jerez de la Frontera, headquarters of the world's sherry trade; Ronda, with its stunning gorge and 18th-century bullring; and Cádiz, considered the oldest city in Spain. Numerous *pueblos blancos* (white villages) dot the landscape of the interior.

It is these Andalucían towns and cities, suggesting those quintessential images, that come to mind when Spain is mentioned – places that are steeped in history, with romantic palaces, flamenco dancers and a sun-drenched landscape.

A BRIEF HISTORY

The southern part of Spain is at a geographical crossroads: It is the gateway between the Mediterranean and the Atlantic, and the crossing point between Africa and Europe. The strategic importance of its location has given rise to a long and turbulent history.

The earliest evidence of human occupation is provided by the Paleolithic cave paintings, some 25,000 years old, in the Cueva de la Pileta. Neolithic peoples arrived on the scene in the 4th millennium BC, leaving behind signs of early attempts at agriculture and fragments of their pottery. Tribes of Iberians from North Africa crossed over into Spain around 3000BC and initiated Spain's first experiments in architecture; Spain's oldest structure stands near Antequera, a dolmen burial chamber known as the Cueva de Romeral. After 900BC, wandering bands of Celts entered the peninsula from northern Europe and brought to the area their knowledge of bronze and iron work. As they moved further south, the Celts merged with the Iberians and began to build walled villages along the coast.

Traders and Colonisers

About the same time that this was taking place, the Phoenicians were already venturing across the Mediterranean from their homeland in present-day Lebanon. They reached Spain by about 1100BC, founding many trading settlements in the land they called *Span* or *Spania*. The first was Gades (modern Cádiz), followed by Malaka (now Málaga) and Abdera (Adra) on the Costa del Sol. Contact with the sophisticated Phoenicians introduced the Celt-Iberians to the concept of currency.

After 650BC, Greek traders entered the competition to exploit Spain's rich mineral deposits and fertile land. Their influence was short-lived, although the olive and the grape, both Greek legacies, soon became important crops.

The Carthaginians, a North African people related to the Phoenicians, subsequently took over much of southern Spain, beginning with Cádiz in 501BC. They extended their influence along the River Guadalquivir to Sevilla, then to Córdoba. On the coast, they founded the city of Carteya, overlooking the Bay of Algeciras (240BC). Carthage, challenged by Rome in the First Punic War (264–241), lost most of its Spanish possessions to Iberian attacks. However, its fortunes changed with an initial victory in the Second Punic War (218–201).

Emboldened, the Carthaginian general Hannibal decided to advance on Rome. He led one of history's great military marches from Spain into Italy, crossing the Pyrenees and the Alps on the way. The Romans invaded Spain to cut off Hannibal's supply route – and stayed there for some 600 years.

The Roman Bridge in Córdoba

Roman Rule

It took the Romans two centuries to subdue the Iberians, but in the end most of the peninsula was incorporated into their new colony of Hispania. The south formed part of the province of Baetica, virtually identical to today's Andalucía, with Córdoba its capital.

The Romans had a far-reaching influence on the country. A road network was constructed (the Via Augusta ran the length of the south coast on its way to Rome) and bridges, aqueducts, villas and public buildings were added to the list of their achievements. The introduction of the Latin language (from which modern Spanish developed), Roman law (the basis of Spain's legal system) and, eventually, Christianity all brought about stability and a degree of unity.

Ultimately the Roman Empire began to crumble and the Romans withdrew from Spain. This left the country to be

Málaga's Alcazaba is a fortified palace built by the Moors

overrun by various barbarian tribes, especially the Vandals. The Visigoths, who controlled much of southern Spain for some 300 years, eventually dominated these tribes, but ultimately the Visigothic kingdom proved unstable. The monarchy was elective, rather than hereditary, which led to disputes over succession. During one of these altercations, the disaffected party looked to North Africa for an ally.

Moors and Christians

In AD711, some 12,000 Berber troops landed at Gibraltar, beginning a period of Moorish rule that was not broken by the Christians until nearly 800 years later. Following their victory at the Battle of Guadalete, the Moors (the name given to the Muslims in Spain) carried all before them. They pushed the Visigoths into the northern mountains and within 10 years most of the country had fallen to Islam.

The Moors chose Córdoba as their seat of government and from the 8th to the very early 11th century, it ranked as one of the great cities of the world. It was capital of the independent caliphate of Córdoba, founded by Abd-ar-Rahman III in 929. Under the caliphs, southern Spain knew prosperity and peace, for the Moors were relatively tolerant rulers and taxed non-believers rather than trying to convert them. Intellectual life flourished and great advances were made in science and medicine.

With the introduction of a sophisticated irrigation system, crops such as rice, cotton and sugar cane were cultivated for the first time on Spanish soil, as were

> To this day, Almuñécar, Tarifa, Algeciras, Benalmádena and several other towns are known by their Arabic names. All place names beginning with the prefix Al- have Moorish origins. Almería's Arabic name, for instance, means 'the mirror of the sea'.

oranges, peaches and pomegranates. The manufacture of paper and glass was another Moorish innovation. Skilled engineers and architects, the Moors built numerous palaces and fortifications. As superb craftsmen they excelled in the production of ceramics and tooled leather, as well as delicate silverware.

The ensuing fall of Córdoba was as remarkable as its rise. In 1009, the caliphate splintered into a number of small kingdoms called *taifas*, which were constantly at war. The Christians in the north, seeing the enemy weakened and divided, captured the *taifa* of Toledo. Under threat of attack, the other *taifas* sought help from the Almoravids, fanatical Berber warriors. The Berbers marched against the Christians in 1086 and went on to reduce Moorish Spain to a province of their own North African Empire.

For a time the affairs of Muslim Spain were administered from the Almoravid headquarters in Granada, until the Almoravids, softened by a life of ease in Andalucía, lost their grip on the peninsula. The pattern repeated itself a century later when the Moors invoked the aid of the Almohads, from the Atlas Mountains of Morocco, in 1151. They soon made themselves the masters of southern Spain and constructed major fortifications, such as Sevilla's Alcázar, endowing the Moors with sufficient strength to resist the Christian forces a while longer.

The fortunes of the Moors and Christians swayed back and forth until 1212, when the Christians gained their

Sevilla's Alcázar, a masterpiece of Moorish architecture

first decisive victory at Las Navas de Tolosa in northern Andalucía. The Christians gradually captured and annexed the former bastions of Moorish rule; in 1236, Córdoba fell to Jaime the Conqueror, followed by Sevilla in 1248. The Moors were in retreat, retrenching along the coast and withdrawing to the security of their strongholds in Ronda and Granada.

In military disarray and political decline, Moorish Spain nevertheless saw another two centuries of brilliance under the Nasrid dynasty, founded in Granada by Mohammed I in 1232. Refugees from Córdoba and Sevilla flooded into

The Alhambra in Granada: the finest memorial to the Nasrids

the city, bringing with them their talents and skills and adding to the city's brilliance. The magnificent palace of the Alhambra provided the setting for a luxurious court life dedicated to the pursuit of literature, music and the arts.

Yet the Moorish fortresses along the coast soon came under attack. Sancho IV took Gibraltar in 1310, but the Christians later relinquished their prize and the Moors held on to it until 1462. In the 1480s the Christians launched a new offensive; Ronda capitulated to the sovereigns Ferdinand and Isabella in 1485, followed by Málaga in 1487 and Almería in 1488. The whole of Christendom gave thanks when Granada was finally conquered in 1492.

The Golden Age

With the triumph of Christianity, the country was united under the Catholic Monarchs *(Los Reyes Católicos)*, a title conferred by Pope Alexander VI on Ferdinand II of Aragón and Isabella I of Castile. Also in 1492, Cristobal Colón (Christopher Columbus) discovered the New World in the name of the Spanish crown. Fanatical in their religious zeal, the king and queen expelled all Jews who refused to convert to Christianity in the same year, followed by the Moors in 1502. The rulers thus reneged on the promise of religious freedom they had given when Granada surrendered. With the Jews who left Spain went many of the country's bankers and merchants, and with the Moors, a good number of its agriculturists and labourers. The converted Jews *(Conversos)* and Moors *(Moriscos)* who remained in Spain were viewed with suspicion by the Inquisition, which had been established by the Catholic Monarchs to stamp out heresy. Many were condemned to death and still more fled the country to escape persecution.

Sevilla's Giralda: converted from a mosque into a Christian bell tower

The 16th century was glorious for Spain, with the conquest of the New World bringing much prestige and wealth. In 1503, the Casa de Contratación in Sevilla was awarded a monopoly on trade with Spain's territories in the Americas. For more than two centuries, Sevilla was the richest city in Spain.

By comparison, coastal settlements languished and were subject to frequent raids by Barbary pirates. Under constant threat for more than 200 years, the population drifted inland, taking refuge in fortified towns and villages hidden in the foothills of the Sierras.

The tomb of Ferdinand and Isabella in the Capilla Real, Granada

Emperor Carlos V of the Holy Roman Empire, the first Habsburg Spanish king, turned his attention to European events. Between 1521 and 1556, he went to war with France four times, squandering the riches of the Americas on endless military campaigns. Carlos also had a weakness for such costly projects as his vast Renaissance palace in the grounds of the Alhambra, which he commissioned in 1526. Taxes imposed on the Moors served to finance the building works, which eventually had to be abandoned for lack of funds when the Moriscos revolted 12 years into the reign of Felipe II (1556–98). The king dispatched his half-brother, Don Juan of Austria, to quell the rebellion, which ended in 1570 with the defeat of the Moriscos and their eventual dispersal. In 1588, Felipe II prepared to invade England, only to be repulsed when the English navy destroyed Spain's previously invincible Armada.

The defeat marked the start of a long decline. Felipe's military forays and his expensive taste left Spain encumbered with debts. Participation in the Thirty Years' War under

Felipe III led to further financial difficulties and to another debacle in 1643, when Spanish troops were defeated by the French at Rocroi in Flanders, never to regain their prestige.

French Ascendancy

Spain's internal affairs became the concern of the other great powers after Carlos II died without an heir. The Habsburg Archduke Charles of Austria challenged the French Philip of Bourbon in the ensuing War of the Spanish Succession. Gibraltar was the scene of some fierce fighting in 1704, when Britain captured the Rock on behalf of Austria. Under the terms of the Treaty of Utrecht, which also confirmed Philip's right to the Spanish throne, Spain was finally forced to relinquish its claims to Gibraltar in 1713.

Nearly 100 years later, during the Napoleonic Wars, Spanish ships fought alongside the French fleet against Lord Nelson at Cape Trafalgar *(see below)*. But as the wars continued, Napoleon, distrustful of his ally, forced the Spanish king Ferdinand VII to abdicate in 1808 and imposed his own brother, Joseph, as king. He then sent thousands of troops across the Pyrenees to subjugate the Spanish, who promptly revolted. Aided by British troops, who were subsequently

The Battle of Trafalgar

Fifty kilometres (30 miles) northwest of Tarifa lies the Cabo de Trafalgar (from the Arabic *Tarif al-Gar*, or Cape of the Cave). Off this headland on 21 October 1805, a British fleet of 27 ships under Admiral Horatio Nelson engaged 33 French and Spanish vessels in one of history's most famous naval battles, which established Britain's naval supremacy for the next 100 years. The enemy was routed, losing nearly two-thirds of its ships. No British vessels were lost, but Nelson was hit by a sniper's bullet and died just before the battle's end.

commanded by the Duke of Wellington, the Spanish drove the French from the Iberian Peninsula. At Tarifa, the enemy was defeated literally overnight in an offensive of 1811. What the world now knows as the Peninsular War (1808–14) is referred to in Spain as the War of Independence. During this troubled period, Spain's first, short-lived, constitution was drafted and Spanish colonies in South America won their independence.

Troubled Times

Ferdinand's return to the throne in 1814 destroyed any hopes left for a constitutional monarchy, but tension between liberals and conservatives led to a century of conflict, marked by the upheavals of the three Carlist wars and the abortive First Republic, which was proclaimed in 1873.

Ramón Narváez is commemorated in his home town of Loja

When Ferdinand died in 1833 his three-year-old daughter María Cristina Isabella was proclaimed queen. Her right to succeed was disputed by supporters of her uncle, Don Carlos, and her succession precipitated the first Carlist war (1833–9).

While Isabella was a child, first her mother then General Baldomero Espartero acted as regents, but in 1843 Espartero was deposed by military officers and Isabella, still only 13, was declared queen in her own right. Her reign, which lasted until 1868, was characterised by political unrest and a series of uprisings. Her government was dominated by military politicians, notably General Ramón María Narváez, Prime Minister several times, and the somewhat more liberal General Leopoldo O'Donnell. Liberal opposition to the regime's authoritarianism became increasingly directed at Isabella. Scandalous reports on the private conduct of the queen, who lived apart from her husband, Francisco de Asís de Borbón, as well as her arbitrary political interference, further damaged the monarchy's cause. An abortive uprising in 1866, and the deaths of O'Donnell and Narváez soon afterwards, weakened her position further. In the autumn of 1868 a successful revolution drove her into exile.

Isabella settled in Paris, where in 1870 she abdicated in favour of her eldest surviving son, Alfonso. After a short-lived republic – Spain's first republican administration – Alfonso ascended the throne in 1874 and monarchy returned to Spain for another 50 years.

On the Andalucían coast, the 19th century was a time of tentative expansion. With piracy at an end, a number of towns and villages grew up along the shoreline and the extension of the railway line to Almería in 1899 promoted the early development of the eastern region.

The Second Republic

Alfonso XIII, just 16 years old, assumed the crown in 1902. Prosperity and stability continued to elude the country, which remained neutral during World War I. Against a murky background of violence, strikes and regional strife, the king accepted the dictatorship of General Miguel Primo de Rivera in 1923. Seven years later, the opposition of radical forces toppled Primo de Rivera from power. King Alfonso went into exile following anti-royalist election results in 1931 and another republic was founded.

Parliamentary elections in 1933 produced a swing to the right and public opinion became polarised. When the left came out on top in the elections of 1936, the situation deteriorated at an alarming rate. It came as no surprise when, six months later, General Francisco Franco led a large section of the army against the socialist government. Support for the Franco-led nationalist uprising came from monarchists, conservatives and the right-wing Falangist organisation, as well as the Roman Catholic Church, while liberals, socialists, communists and anarchists sided with the government.

The bloodshed of the Spanish Civil War lasted for three years and cost hundreds of thousands of lives. Franco emerged as the leader of a shattered Spain. Many republicans went into exile; others simply disappeared. (The republican mayor of Mijas caused a sensation when he surfaced in the 1960s after three decades in hiding – in his own home.) Franco kept the impoverished country out of World War II, despite Hitler's entreaties. The Spanish nation gradually healed its wounds, though conditions were extremely difficult for many years and life was a struggle for many people.

Italian planes bomb the Republicans in the Civil War

Changing Fortunes

All that was to change when Spain's tourist potential began to be exploited in the late 1950s. Credit was made available for hotel and apartment development and former fishing villages like Torremolinos and Marbella began to change forever. Spain's admission to the United Nations in 1955, followed by the advent of jet travel and package holidays in the 1960s, subsequently opened up the coast to mass tourism.

With the death of Franco in 1975, Spain became a democracy. The monarchy was restored in the person of King Juan Carlos, the grandson of Alfonso XIII. More than just a figurehead, the king helped to thwart a military coup in 1981, keeping Spain firmly on a democratic course. A process of decentralisation was begun, with powers being devolved to 17 semi-autonomous regions and on 28 February 1982, Andalucía was given autonomous status.

In the same year, the PSOE, the socialist government of Felipe González, was elected and committed itself to Spain's integration into the European Community, now the European Union. As a precondition of admission, the border with Gibraltar was reopened in February 1985, after a 16-year hiatus and Spain joined the EC in 1986. In 1992 Sevilla hosted Expo '92, and investment poured into Andalucía. The PSOE lost power in 1996, to be replaced by the centre-right Partido Popular under José María Aznar. Socialist mayors still dominate in Andalucía, but their economic and structural plans are supported by central government in Madrid.

Juan Carlos became king after Franco's death in 1975

Historical Landmarks

circa **3000BC** Iberian tribes migrate to Spain from North Africa.

1100BC Phoenicians found coastal settlements.

900BC Celts wander south from northern Europe.

650BC Greek traders found a series of colonies.

2nd century BC Romans conquer Spain.

5th century AD Visigothic kingdom established.

711 Moors launch their conquest of Spain.

929 Caliphate of Córdoba founded.

11th–12th centuries The caliphate splinters into small kingdoms called *taifas*.

1212 Christians defeat Moors at Las Navas de Tolosa.

1232 Nasrid dynasty founded in Granada.

1492 Granada falls to Ferdinand and Isabella. Christopher Columbus discovers America.

16th century Emperor Carlos V and King Felipe II expand Spain's empire during the Golden Age.

1609 The Moors are finally expelled from Spain.

1704 Great Britain captures Gibraltar.

1808 Napoleon sets his brother, Joseph, on the Spanish throne, triggering the War of Independence (1808–14).

1873 Proclamation of Spain's first (short-lived) republic.

1902–31 Political unrest grows under King Alfonso XIII.

1936–39 Spanish Civil War: at least 600,000 die.

1939–75 Dictatorship of General Francisco Franco.

1975 Spain becomes a constitutional monarchy.

1982 Andalucía is given autonomous status, with its own president and parliament.

1986 Spain enters European Union (then the EC).

1992 Sevilla hosts Expo '92. High-speed train link (the AVE) established, cutting journey time to Madrid to two hours.

1996 Partido Popular, under José María Aznar, gains power.

2002 The euro replaces the peseta as the currency of Spain.

WHERE TO GO

GETTING AROUND

Most visitors to the Costa del Sol are based in one of the large coastal resorts to the west of Málaga (Torremolinos, Benalmádena, Fuengirola, Marbella or Estepona), while far fewer head east towards Nerja, Almuñécar, or even as far as Almería. Although the main aim for many is to relax on the beach and soak up as much sun as possible, increasing numbers arrive to play golf. It comes as little surprise, therefore, that the road signs proclaim the area west of Málaga not just as the *Costa del Sol,* but also the *Costa del Golf.*

A few visitors forsake the beach for a day or two and venture out to the amazingly varied historic towns and cities or to the natural wonders of the national parks nearby. Málaga, Ronda and perhaps Gibraltar can be visited in a day, but a trip to Sevilla, Córdoba, Granada or the national parks necessitates at least an overnight stop.

MÁLAGA

Málaga's international airport is the gateway to the Costa del Sol and Andalucía for most people. However, few visitors spend much time in the city itself. This is a shame, because Málaga is an ancient Andalucían city of considerable charm that offers a refreshing taste of the real Spain.

Founded by Phoenician traders more than 3,000 years ago, it came under Carthaginian and Roman rule before falling to the Moorish invasion force in 711. The Moors fortified the city, developing the settlement into a major trading port serving Granada, and it was one of the last cities in Spain to be reconquered by Christian forces in 1487.

The famous cathedral in Sevilla is Europe's third largest church

A good place to begin a tour is at Málaga's principal land-mark, the **Castillo del Gibralfaro** (from the Arabic *Jebel al Faro* – Lighthouse Hill). Located some 130m (425ft) above the city, this hill is capped by the ramparts of a Phoenician castle reconstructed in the 14th century by the Moors, who went on to build the lighthouse that gave Gibralfaro its name. The restored walls and parapets offer a superb panoramic view of both the city below and the coastline disappearing into the horizon. Because it looks down on the Plaza de Toros, the hill also acts as free seating for bullfight enthusiasts.

It is possible to walk up here but it is not recommended. It's a steep climb, the pathway is somewhat difficult in places and it's a well-known hangout for muggers. Best to take a taxi or a bus from the delightful **Paseo del Parque**, with contrasting fountains at either end, which connects the old town with the Plaza de Toros. On its south side, it is a lush seaside tropical garden enhanced by fountains, duck ponds and small bars. The other side is home to the smaller Jardínes Puerta Oscura and two impressive buildings, the Ayuntamiento (Town Hall) and the 18th-century La Aduana (Old Custom House).

Immediately behind is the **Alcazaba**, a sprawling, fortified palace complex built by the Moors. A cobbled path climbs up the hillside within the walls to the Arco del Cristo (Gateway of Christ). The victorious Christian army of Ferdinand and Isabella celebrated Mass here when the fortress finally fell into their hands in

> **Málaga's vast cathedral is known locally as La Manquita – the one-armed lady – because only one of its twin towers was completed. The north tower soars 100m (330ft) above the street, but work on the other, a forlorn stump of stone, stopped in 1783 because of a lack of money.**

The 14th-century Castillo del Gilbralfaro looks down on Málaga

1487. Higher still, the palace itself contains a small archaeological museum. Beside the entrance to the Alcazaba are the partially excavated ruins of the **Teatro Romano**, the only visible remains of the Roman city.

Málaga was the birthplace, in 1881, of Pablo Ruiz Picasso, although the artist left his native city at the age of 14 for Madrid and Barcelona. The house where he was born, **Casa Natal Picasso** (open Tues–Sat 10am–2pm, 6–9pm, Sun 10am–2pm) at Plaza de la Merced 14, is a small museum, reference library and headquarters of the Picasso Foundation. On a much grander scale, the **Museo Picasso** (open Mon–Sat 9am–9pm, Sun 9am–2pm), housed in the renovated and expanded Palacio de los Condes de Buenavista, opened in 2003. As well as displaying about 200 of Picasso's works, the museum highlights the history of the city.

The **Museo de Artes y Tradiciones Populares** (open Mon–Fri 10am–1.30pm, 5–8pm, Sat 10am–1.30pm) in the

**Fresh local produce in
the Mercado Atarazanas**

Posada de la Victoria, a 17th-century inn on the western edge of the old town, offers a fascinating glimpse into how life was lived in Málaga in generations past.

On the way back to the centre of Málaga, stop for a moment or two at the neo-Mudéjar building housing the **Mercado Atarazanas** (market). Each morning it is filled with women admiring the bountiful displays of meat, fish, fruit and vegetables, and shopping for fresh, not plastic-wrapped, produce. This is also the western boundary of a collection of small roads and pedestrianised streets that end at the main street, Calle Marqués de Larios, and combine to form Málaga's principal shopping centre. You can buy almost anything here, from foodstuffs to footwear, but remember that the siesta still reigns in this part of Spain and nothing is open in the afternoon between about 2pm and 5pm.

North of Málaga

Just an hour's drive north of Málaga lies some magnificent mountain scenery. The national park of **El Torcal de Antequera** is a high limestone plateau that has been eroded by rainwater into a fantasy landscape of fluted pinnacles and towers. Hikers can explore the marked trails, which are up to 5km (3 miles) long and wind among the rocks. There are panoramic views back to Málaga and the distant Mediterranean.

Near the town of Álora, you will find the breathtaking 300-m (1,000-ft) deep gorge known as **La Garganta del Chorro**. This sheer-sided canyon is cut by the Río Guadalhorce. It is also accessible from Málaga by train; just ask for a ticket to El Chorro. An improbable concrete catwalk called the Camino del Rey (The King's Way) crosses a vertical cliff and continues into the heart of the gorge, a dizzying 65m (200ft) above the river. It was built in the 1920s to provide access for workers digging tunnels for a hydroelectric project. The dams above the gorge have created attractive lakes, known as the **Pantanos del Chorro**. Fringed with woods, sandy beaches and campsites, they are a refreshing change of scenery from the heat and bustle of the coast.

Finding Your Way Around

derecha	right	**iglesia**	church
izquierda	left	**isla**	island
todo derecho	straight ahead	**jardín**	garden
alcázar	fortress	**mercado**	market
ascensor	lift	**mezquita**	mosque
autopista	motorway	**muelle**	docks
avenida	avenue	**murallas**	ramparts
ayuntamiento	town hall	**museo**	museum
barrio	quarter	**oficina de**	tourist
cabo	cape	**turismo**	office
calle	street	**paseo**	boulevard
camino	highway	**playa**	beach
carretera	road	**plaza**	square
castillo	castle	**plaza de**	bullring
ciudad vieja	old town	**toros**	
correos	post office	**puerto**	harbour
cueva	cave	**río**	river
estación de	railway	**sierra**	mountain
ferrocarril	station		range
faro	lighthouse	**vía**	avenue

WEST OF MÁLAGA

Some of Europe's most popular beach resorts line the coast that stretches 160km (100 miles) to the Rock of Gibraltar.

Torremolinos

Just a few kilometres west of Málaga's international airport lies **Torremolinos**. In the late 1950s and early 1960s, it was the first resort on the Costa del Sol to establish a reputation as a popular international playground. Although little more than an overgrown village, it was a haven for young northern Europeans seeking an inexpensive holiday with sun, sand and sangría.

Calle San Miguel, the busy main street of Torremolinos

Since then, it has built, quite literally, on that reputation. Although it is nowhere near as inexpensive as it once was, it is still a highly popular tourist destination, with accommodation for some 130,000 visitors – much of it in high-rise blocks. Wall-to-wall hotels and apartments reach back in rows from the beaches and there's no denying that it delivers everything sun-hungry visitors could wish for. Miles of glorious beaches, cheap alcohol and familiar food, numerous bars, discos and nightclubs attract a clientele that is largely British, although

Germans, Scandinavians and others also arrive in large numbers. This international invasion has completely overwhelmed the town and foreign languages are more dominant than Spanish.

Although the first mention of Torremolinos dates back to 1498, there is really nothing here of historical signifi-cance. The town itself, espe-cially **Calle San Miguel**, is simply a profusion of shops.

High-rise hotels line the Torremolinos beaches

At the bottom of San Miguel a series of winding stairways leads down towards a 7-km (4-mile) sweep of golden coast-line. This consists of six **beaches** connected by the Paseo Marí-timo (beach promenade) and broken only by the rocky promontory of Castillo de Santa Clara, which separates the Ba-jondillo (east) and Carihuela (west) sections of town.

Chiringuitos (small beachside restaurants) are in plentiful supply, especially in the former fishing village of **La Cari-huela**. There are still a few bona fide fishermen about and if you drag yourself out of bed between 6am and 8am, you'll see them returning in their gaily painted, flat-bottomed wooden boats, with nets of sardines and anchovies. At lunchtime, you can sample the morning's catch, skewered on a wooden stick and grilled over a fire on the beach.

Many other popular attractions lie close at hand, including the wave pools and water slides of Atlantis Aquapark, the horse show at the Club El Rancho and the 18-hole course of the nearby Parador del Golf. But the biggest draw in Torre-molinos are the bars and clubs that have earned the resort its reputation for noisy, non-stop nightlife.

Benalmádena-Costa

Heading west it appears, at first glance, that Benalmádena-Costa is indistinguishable from its close neighbour, but this isn't really so. It is somewhat less built up and frenetic than Torremolinos, even though it's well endowed with bars, discos and clubs. Its fine beaches stretch for 9km (5 miles), beginning at the large and attractive Puerto Deportivo on the border with Torremolinos. Focal points are the three Moorish watchtowers; the pink, mock-Moorish walls of **Castillo de Bil-Bil**, built by a Frenchwoman in the 1930s and used for concerts, exhibitions and as a tourist office; and one of the Costa del Sol's casinos in the huge and impressive Torrequebrada complex.

Two kilometres (1 mile) inland and high above the sea lies the pretty, whitewashed village of **Benalmádena**. Its **Museo Arqueológico y de Arte Colombiano** (open Tues–Sat 10am–2pm, 4–7pm) takes pride in a collection of pre-Columbian art (said to be the most important of its kind in Spain), with jewellery, statuary and ceramics from Mexico and Central America. Also in the Benalmádena area is the **Tívoli World** amusement park, in Arroyo de la Miel *(see page 92)*, the **Sea Life** aquarium in the Puerto Deportivo and **Eagle Park** at the Castillo de Colomares.

One of Benalmádena-Costa's three Moorish watchtowers

Fuengirola

Located 9km (6 miles) down the road, Fuengirola is another resort that's hugely popular with the English. Here bacon and eggs, fish and chips, darts, snooker,

On the beach in Fuengirola

English beer and bars showing football matches on television are the norm. But Fuengirola has assimilated this without losing all its Spanish character. This is particularly true in early October, during the annual fair, when the town becomes a blaze of colour and noise and almost every man, woman and child dons typical Andalucían dress. Tradition survives, too, in the commercial fishing fleet, which is an ongoing concern.

The Plaza de la Constitución in the town centre has numerous pleasant cafés lining the square beneath the church bell tower, and nearby is the bullring and the small **Zoologico Municipal** (Zoo). Across the river at the western end of town rise the remains of the **Castillo de Sohail**. Abder-Rahman III built this hilltop fortress in the 10th century and gradually a settlement grew up around the walls. Taken by the Christians in a bloody battle in 1487, Sohail was then levelled on the orders of the Catholic Monarchs. After it was rebuilt, it was occupied during the Peninsular War by French troops who left behind a souvenir of their stay – the cannon that are now displayed along the promenade of the **Paseo Marítimo**. Other attractions here include a variety of water sports, a marina, the fishing harbour, a sailing school, the waterslides of the Mijas Aqua Park, the El Cartujano horse show and horse racing at the Mijas Hippodrome.

Mijas

Clinging to the hillside 8km (5 miles) inland from Fuengirola is **Mijas**. Surrounded by modern villas and *urbanizaciones* (developments), it looks from the outside like any other quaint village with whitewashed houses. But Mijas is different. Most of the houses have been converted into upmarket shops, restaurants or bars, making the whole village a tourist attraction. Traffic is banned from the centre, so if you don't feel like the short walk from the car park, you will have to take a mule taxi.

Mijas has Spain's only square **bullring** and, opposite, beautifully tended gardens slope down to a cliff-top mirador, with fine views all along the coast. There is another viewpoint beside the car park. On one side of this natural balcony you will find a tiny **chapel** dedicated to La Virgen de la Peña, set in a grotto carved from living rock. The Virgin is celebrated in a lively festival in September.

Marbella

Sheltered by the mountains of the Sierra Blanca on one side and with the Mediterranean on the other, Marbella has earned a reputation for being the most aristocratic of Costa del Sol's resorts. This began in the 1950s when Prince Alfonso von Hohenlohe bought land and built himself a luxurious home here. It became so popular with his guests that he developed it into the Marbella Club Hotel and that in turn launched Marbella as a trendy gathering place for the jet set in the 1960s. Today the town is still a playground for the rich and famous, frequented by celebrities and politicians, royalty and business tycoons. As a consequence, it has promoted the further development, both here and along the coast, of the largest collection of luxury hotels in Spain. Naturally, prices are much higher here than in the other coastal resorts, but you get what you pay for in terms of superior standards of accommodation, service and cuisine.

Marbella is a town in two distinct parts. The largest by far is the modern section and the centre of this, clustered around the palm trees and fountains of the Parque de la Alameda, is taken up with busy pavement cafés, smart boutiques, banks and estate agents' offices. The construction of a four-lane bypass has put an end to the crush of traffic that used to jam this part of town.

The elegant Iglesia de la Encarnación in Marbella

It is at its most attractive, though, by the sea, where the municipality of Marbella encompasses some 28km (17 miles) of beachfront. The promenade winds along the beaches of El Fuerte and Fontanilla, passing Puerto Deportivo, a **marina** with moorings for several hundred pleasure boats, overlooked by the tall spire of the lighthouse. Some lively beach bars and restaurants make this a popular part of town.

The promenade extends west for a mile or two, between attractive apartment complexes and long stretches of golden sands. The monuments of modern Marbella cling to the hills on the western outskirts. The King of Saudi Arabia's holiday home – it looks a bit like the White House in Washington, only slightly larger – hides behind a row of pines and palms on a hilltop just above the highway, surrounded by high security fences. On a neighbouring hill stands Marbella's modern-style mosque, the Mezquita del Rey Abdulaziz Al Saud (open every afternoon except Friday).

> **Visitors with a fascination for very small trees should visit Marbella's Museo del Bonsai (open Tues–Sun 10am–1.30pm, 4–7pm), the only one in Spain and one of the best in the world.**

But Marbella has its historic side, too. In fact, its history goes back some 1,600 years, even though most of what can be seen, in the town at least, dates from the time of the Catholic Monarchs or later. North of the main road, the **Casco Antiguo** (Old Town) provides an intriguing glimpse of the past, cleverly integrated to cater to modern visitors. First, sit at a café table in the **Plaza de los Naranjos** (Square of the Orange Trees), where you can admire the noble 16th-century façade of the **Ayuntamiento** (Town Hall) and soak up the atmosphere. Then wander through the maze of narrow, twisting streets where the whitewashed walls are decorated with colourful baskets of flowers.

As you explore the neighbourhood, you'll come across the historic parish church with a landmark bell tower and the convents of La Trinidad and San Francisco (it is said that Miguel de Cervantes, creator of Don Quixote, lodged at the latter). Uphill from the church lie the crumbling walls of the Moorish *castillo*. Scattered throughout this area is an eclectic array of shops and galleries. The **Museum of**

Contemporary Spanish Prints (tel: 952 825 035 for hours), housed in the old Bazán Hospital, contains works by Picasso, Miró, Tapies and other renowned artists.

Just outside Marbella are three other places with ancient historical connections: the **Roman Villa mosaics** dating from the 1st and 2nd centuries at Río Verde near the beach; the Paleo-Christian basilica, **Vega del Mar**, in San Pedro de Alcántara; and **Las Bovedas** (The Cellars), the Roman baths at Guadalmina.

With the increasing popularity of Marbella, high society has moved west to the chic suburb of Nueva Andalucía and its magnificent harbour, **Puerto Banús**. Sleek, unbelievably expensive yachts line the quayside, and Porsches, Rolls-Royces and Mercedes fill the streets. There's a glamorous line-up of expensive restaurants and high-class boutiques that seem to be permanently open. High rollers haunt the

Puerto Banús provides moorings for seriously expensive yachts

tables in the nearby Casino Marbella, then sip martinis and watch the sun rise from the decks of their luxury yachts. Even if you can't afford to join in, it's fun just to watch how the other half lives. If you prefer to watch fish, the aquarium in Puerto Banús is small, but nonetheless interesting.

This part of the Costa del Sol is also a golfer's paradise. There are 30 golf clubs in operation between Málaga and Sotogrande. These courses cater to all levels, from beginners to professionals taking part in some of the important competitions in the tour calendar. At least half a dozen quality courses can be found between the western edge of Marbella and San Pedro de Alcántara.

Extensive white, sandy beaches first drew tourists to Marbella

Ojén

Inland from Marbella lie the high peaks of the Sierra Blanca, the most distinctive being La Concha (The Seashell), which rises directly above the town. A scenic road leads to the village of **Ojén** (famous for *aguardiente,* a fierce anise spirit produced here) and on to the mountain pass called Puerto de Ojén. Just beyond, a road on the left leads to the **Refugio de Juanar**, a hunting lodge set at the heart of a large national game reserve. The peace and tranquillity found here has attracted numerous personalities, among them General Charles de Gaulle of France, who finished his memoirs here in 1970.

Estepona

The last major resort town on the western part of the Costa del Sol provides all the holiday essentials – good beaches, restaurants, golf courses and a marina – with a small-town atmosphere.

A sunny balcony in Estepona

Low-rise apartment blocks, unpretentious restaurants and hotels overlook the palm-lined **Paseo Marítimo**, a promenade furnished with park benches, flower displays and a little playground.

Originally a Roman settlement, Estepona preserves the remains of Moorish fortifications and watchtowers, an 18th-century parish church and an expressionistic bullring, a startling piece of modern architecture that is beginning to look rather the worse for wear. On either side of the town itself, gracious and upmarket hotels are beginning to make an impression on the coastline.

Beyond Estepona, development is more sporadic, although there are some luxury resorts at Sotogrande and Puerto Duquesa. About 6km (4 miles) outside town, a mountain road takes you up to **Casares**, a spectacular white hilltop village clinging precariously to the rugged slopes below its Moorish fort. The road, lined with eucalyptus trees, commands sweeping views of the coast and countryside, and on a clear day the eye is inevitably drawn to the twin peaks known in ancient times as the Pillars of Hercules – the Rock of Gibraltar on the right and Morocco's Jebel Musa on the left.

The Rock of Gibraltar, once thought to be the edge of the world

Gibraltar looms ever larger as you approach **San Roque**, which was established by Spanish refugees who fled the Rock when the English captured it in 1704. Building blocks for the town were found, conveniently, in the nearby ruins of Roman Carteya (little remains today of the classical site). Branch off the main road here and head for **La Línea de la Concepción** and the Rock itself. La Línea has experienced a mini-boom since the border with Gibraltar was reopened in 1985 after a blockade lasting 16 years, but is still a dreary place.

Gibraltar

Gibraltar was a home for pre-historic man: neanderthal skulls were found in 1848 and 1928 and this is considered one of the final bastions for this species. Although it is known that the Phoenicians, Greeks and Carthaginians were aware of Gibraltar and that the Romans controlled the region from about 500BC to AD475, no town was ever built. The

Visigoths and Vandals destroyed almost all traces of culture in the area and it wasn't until long after the Moors invaded, in 711 that the first city was constructed. However, even that wasn't completed until nearly 450 years later, in 1160.

The next three centuries saw numerous battles and it was not until 1462 that Gibraltar was finally reconquered by the Spanish. In the early 18th century, problems over succession to the Spanish throne led to an Anglo-Dutch force capturing Gibraltar in 1704. Under the Treaty of Utrecht in 1713 Spain ceded its rights to Gibraltar to the British – although the Spanish didn't give up without a fight. In 1727, the first siege failed and in 1779 combined Spanish and French forces totalling 50,000 laid the final Great Siege against just 5,000 defenders. It ended after four years of hardship. In 1830 Gibraltar achieved the status of a British Crown Colony, which it still holds. It

Entering Gibraltar

If you arrive by car (Gibraltar is only two hours' drive from Málaga), you have two choices, neither of which is ideal. It is easier and often much faster to leave the car in one of the car parks in La Linea and cross the border on foot. Once in Gibraltar, a car is a hindrance in the town centre and only really useful if you want to take a tour of the Upper Rock. However, the downside of this strategy is the risk of having your car broken into in La Linea. If you want to take your vehicle with you, bear in mind that there is a strong possibility that you will be subject to long delays in either direction. The Spanish authorities, in their ongoing battle with Britain over the sovereignty of Gibraltar, have decided to make the border formalities long and tedious by checking everything and everyone. Beyond the customs area, access to Gibraltar is across the middle of the airport runway (the road has to be closed when aircraft land and take off), then past the defensive walls to the town centre.

Gibraltar is the only place in Europe to see wild Barbary apes

remains the subject of a dispute between the British and Spanish governments.

The town and harbour lie on the east slope of the Rock, overlooking the bay, with the narrow defile of **Main Street** cutting through the middle. This is lined with duty-free shops selling liquor, perfume, cameras, CD players, video recorders and other electronic goods, and English-style pubs serving pints of bitter and bar lunches. The unit of currency is the Gibraltarian pound (equal to the British pound), but shops and other businesses accept both sterling and euros.

Also at sea level is the **Gibraltar Museum** (open Mon–Fri 10am–6pm, Sat 10am–2pm), housed in a building containing what are considered the best-preserved Moorish baths in Europe. The museum has interesting exhibits on Gibraltar's history. Of interest, too, is **Nelson's Anchorage**, where Admiral Nelson's body is said to have been brought in a barrel of rum after the Battle of Trafalgar in October 1805, and the nearby 100-tonne Victorian super-gun, the largest of its type in the world.

Main Street ends at the Referendum Gates, and beyond lies the **cable-car station**, where you can take a trip to the top of the Rock, with a stop halfway to visit the **Apes' Den**. The so-called Barbary apes (actually tailless macaque monkeys) that inhabit the Rock are natives of North Africa, descended from animals brought over by sailors as pets and ships' mascots. Legend has it that if the apes ever leave the Rock, then British rule will come to an end. When the apes' population declined significantly during World War II, Winston Churchill was worried and the monkeys have been on special rations ever since. The views from the summit 426m (1,400ft) up are spectacular, particularly across the strait to Morocco, along the coast towards Estepona and down the sheer east face of the Rock to the water-holding areas (for desalination) and the beaches of Sandy Bay, Catalan Bay and Eastern Beach.

Don't leave Gibraltar without taking a tour of the **Upper Rock Nature Reserve** area. On the way up note the yellow patches and their accompanying metal rings; these were used when manually hauling the heavy cannon up the Rock. Also of interest is the fact that there is no soil on the Upper Rock; the 600 species of wildflower here grow directly out of the limestone from which the Rock is formed.

First stop is **St Michael's Cave** (open daily 9.30am–7.30pm), an impressive natural grotto that is sometimes used as a venue for musical performances. Then stop to see the apes, and at the north end of the Rock, take time to explore the **Upper Galleries**, a system of tunnels blasted through the inside of the rock face during the 18th-century Great Siege. Note that the cannon emplacements slope down-

Main Street, Gibraltar

Tarifa's west-facing beach attracts windsurfers from far and wide

wards, a clever innovation that allowed the defenders to fire directly at the Spanish and French forces attacking from La Linea. What cannot be seen is the 51km (32 miles) of tunnels that were excavated during World War II. It was from these that General Eisenhower conducted the Allied invasion of North Africa. On the way back to town lies the **Moorish castle** which, apart from its 14th-century tower, is of little interest.

Algeciras

Just across the bay from Gibraltar is an uninspiring port town whose only saving grace, on good days at least, is its unsurpassed views of the Rock. From the harbour, hydrofoils and car ferries cross the strait to Ceuta, a Spanish protectorate in North Africa, and to Tangier in Morocco. A day trip to Ceuta is certainly possible, but there is not much of interest there, beyond shopping. Much more interesting and exciting is to continue on about 40km (25 miles) to Tetuan in Morocco, parts of which seem to have remained unchanged for centuries. Because of the two-hour time difference between Ceuta and Morocco, it's difficult, but possible, to see it in one day, so an overnight stop in Ceuta is recommended.

Tarifa

This is where the waters of the Mediterranean mingle with those of the Atlantic and bring the Costa del Sol to an end. Europe looks across the Strait of Gibraltar to Africa, with the Rif Mountains of Morocco dominating the horizon a mere 13km (8 miles) away. A section of the old Moorish walls remains, as does the 10th-century fortress.

However, it is not its history that attracts most visitors these days. The beaches stretching to the west are such a mecca for windsurfers and kitesurfers that Tarifa is often called the windsurf capital of Europe. The prevailing wind, known as the *poniente,* is from the west, making the beaches among the windiest in Europe.

The windsurfers are not the only ones to take advantage of the reliable breeze; the hillsides above the town have sprouted a forest of wind-powered electricity turbines. In spring and autumn, storks, buzzards and other soaring birds fill the skies as they climb in the rising thermals before gliding across the strait on their annual migration, congregating here where the sea crossing is at its shortest.

Alleyway in Tarifa

EAST OF MÁLAGA

The eastern part of the Costa del Sol stretches for more than 200km (125 miles) from Málaga to Almería. This part of the coast has a different feel from the western section, with less intensive development and, in parts, a much rockier and more attractive shoreline.

Málaga to Nerja

Leaving the suburbs of Málaga, you arrive immediately in **Rincón de la Victoria**, a resort largely given over to weekend apartments owned by Spanish city-dwellers. But prehistoric man was here

The white houses of Nerja

first, occupying the **Cueva del Tesoro** (Treasure Cave) on the Málaga side of the town. Cave paintings and prehistoric remains, including a shrine to the goddess Noctiluca, have been discovered, and there is a beautiful underground lake with stalactites. According to legend, five Moorish kings buried a huge treasure inside the cave, but it has never been found.

Torre del Mar is the gateway to the wine and grape region of the Axarquía, and its capital, **Vélez-Málaga**, which lies 4km (2½ miles) inland. Founded by the Phoenicians, Vélez sprawls around an historic centre dominated by a Moorish *alcazaba* and two venerable churches: the late-Gothic Iglesia de San Juan Bautista and the Iglesia de Santa María (which incorporates a section of the town's former mosque).

The village of **Torrox-Costa**, as elsewhere on the eastern Costa, has more self-catering accommodation than hotels. Once dedicated to fishing and agriculture, it has extensive Roman ruins, but is now an expanding resort with a tourism-based economy.

Nerja

Nerja is the one large international resort to the east of Málaga and it's a popular destination for British, German and Scandinavian visitors. Despite the intensive development in the hills surrounding it, the town has managed to retain some of its village atmosphere. The nightlife is pretty lively, though quieter than in Torremolinos, and the beaches, which are tucked into rocky coves, are prettier, if somewhat smaller. The area also offers good opportunities for hiking, horse riding, scuba diving, snorkelling and angling, giving Nerja the edge for those seeking an active holiday.

Hotels and restaurants cluster around the **Balcón de Europa**, a palm-fringed clifftop promenade jutting out over the sea, dividing the sandy crescent of La Caletilla beach on the west from La Calahonda on the east.

Just 6km (4 miles) east of the beach of **Maro** is the famous **Cueva de Nerja** (Cave of Nerja). This huge cavern was discovered in 1959 when a group of local boys stumbled on it one day while they were out hunting bats. Floodlights illuminate the impressive limestone formations, which include a stalagmite/stalactite over 32m (105ft) high and 18m

Stalactites in the Cueva de Nerja

(59ft) in diameter. On display are archaeological remains confirming that these caves were inhabited 30,000 years ago. The Nerja Festival of Music and Dance, held in early July, takes place in the Sala de la Cascada, which has wonderful acoustics. Nearby an attractive aqueduct stands as testimony to the creative skills of the region's earlier generations.

Inland from Nerja, the corrugated hills of the Sierra de Tejeda rise up toward the village of **Frigiliana**. Under the Moors, it was one of the many prosperous villages within the Kingdom of Granada. Today, the historic centre is regarded as an outstanding example of Moorish village architecture, with a lovely 16th-century church and ruined Moorish castle.

The Far East

After Nerja, the scenery changes dramatically; the mountains begin to cascade to the sea and the panoramas of the ragged coastline are magnificent. Just before La Herradura, a neat little town with a nice beach, road signs proclaim that you are now in the Provincia de Granada. Until you pass into Almería, this part of the Costa del Sol, the most attractive but least known, is officially called the Costa Tropical.

Almuñécar is the first town of any size and has an ancient history. A fine **aqueduct** stands as a monument to the skills of the Roman engineers who constructed it during the reign of Antoninus Pius in the 2nd century AD. A port for Granada in Moorish times, Almuñécar continued to enjoy a certain prestige after the Reconquest when Juan de Herrera, the architect of El Escorial, Philip II's grand monastery-cum-palace near Madrid, was commissioned to design the parish church. These days the town, set around an attractive curving beach, is an increasingly popular family resort.

Along the road from Almuñécar, pretty villas with spectacular coastal views dot the hillsides until, all of a sudden, the scenery changes dramatically. As the coast flattens out, a town of whitewashed houses atop a rocky, cone-shaped hill comes into view. Called **Salobreña**, it makes for an impressive sight. A Moorish castle, beautifully restored, stands isolated at the heart of the village.

Salobreña stands as the gateway to the agriculturally rich *vega* (plain) of the thriving port city of **Motril**. Sugar cane, the source of the greenery, flourishes here. The sugar refineries in the area have earned the town its nickname – Little Cuba. Like Cuba, Motril is known for its rum, although its residents are crafty enough to make just about enough for local consumption and no more. Motril and Salobreña have their own extensive beaches and there are many more to come as the road continues eastward.

Salobreña and its castle

The next 40km (25 miles) is a conservation area and the least developed of any section of the coast. The small towns and villages, reminiscent of what the rest of the Costa used to be like before the tourist invasion, have only a few hotels, which means that even in midsummer, the beaches are far from overcrowded. What's more, it's possible to be swimming in the Mediterranean while the snow-covered peaks of the Sierra Nevada shimmer in the distance.

This scenery changes, and much for the worse, after **Adra**, an important fishing and fish processing centre.

The N340/E15 crosses a vast and dreary plain where every available piece of level land has been covered by ugly plastic greenhouses that produce a great deal of Europe's winter vegetables. The road rejoins the coast at **Aguadulce** where tourists, mainly Spanish, enjoy good beaches, new golf courses and marinas. Here, the mountains meet the sea again and the journey on to Almería is short but attractive.

Almería

Rich in history, **Almería** was once the most important city in Moorish Spain. The Almería of today is a pleasant, provincial capital that's worth a visit if your travels take you to the eastern limits of the Costa del Sol.

There are two major sights. One is Abd-er-Rahman III's massive **Alcazaba**, which looms large on the hilltop above the city. Although an earthquake caused extensive damage in

Almería's imposing Alcazaba was built by the first Caliph of Córdoba

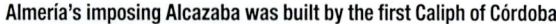

1522, the crenellated ochre walls and a section of the turreted ramparts stood firm, and now provide wide-ranging vistas over the city and the sea. The second is the forbidding, fortified **cathedral** that stands just inland from the waterfront Paseo de Almería. It was built in the 16th century, when Barbary pirates were terrorising the coast.

Inland from Almería lies one of the most un-European landscapes on the European continent. The **Sierra de Alhamilla** is a desert of barren mountains, rocky ravines and dry gravel riverbeds; spiky agave plants and prickly pears are the only vegetation. The region's uncanny resemblance to the American West made it a popular film location for spaghetti westerns, including such classics as *A Fistful of Dollars* and *The Good, the Bad and the Ugly*, which set a young Clint Eastwood on the road to stardom in Hollywood. Near the village of Tabernas is an area known as **Mini-Hollywood**, where two of the film sets have been preserved as tourist attractions, complete with horses, cowboys and barroom brawls.

INLAND EXCURSIONS

For a complete contrast to the sun, sea and sangría atmosphere of the coast, you need only drive inland for a few hours to reach the cultural, historical and architectural attractions of Ronda, Jerez de la Frontera, Sevilla, Córdoba and Granada – the great cities of Andalucía. If time is limited, try taking one of the day trips that are offered in all the major resorts; or focus your attention on Ronda. Most of the other destinations require an overnight stay.

Ronda

The opening of an improved road from San Pedro de Alcántara to **Ronda** has ended the isolation of this mountain area and shortened the driving time from the coast to an hour.

One of the most spectacularly situated towns in Europe, Ronda sits atop a cliff-bound plateau, cleaved through the middle by a sheer-sided gorge. The older, Moorish part of town (La Ciudad) lies to the south of the ravine, linked by an 18th-century bridge to El Mercadillo, the more modern district that arose after the Christian reconquest.

The gorge, known as **El Tajo**, is a deep and narrow crevasse that plunges 150m (490ft) to the foaming Río Guadalevín, a tributary of the Guadiaro. You can enjoy a superb view of the Tajo and the patchwork of fields beyond from the **Puente Nuevo** (New Bridge), built in 1788, and from the walkways that follow the edge of the gorge.

During the Spanish Civil War, nationalist sympathisers in Ronda were hurled to their deaths in the gorge, an event recalled by Ernest Hemingway in his novel *For Whom the Bell Tolls*.

To see some of Ronda's most important monuments, cross the bridge into **La Ciudad**, the old Moorish enclave which remained impervious to Christian assault until 1485. On one side of the Plaza de Campillo square stands the **Palacio de Mondragón**, constructed by Abomelic, King of Ronda, in 1314 and later taken over by the Christian conquerors. A distinguished Renaissance portal, a later addition, opens onto spacious courtyards where horseshoe arches, Arabic inscriptions and distinctive tile ornaments indicate the Moorish origins of this grand building.

A block or so away, Ronda's original mosque survives in the form of the **Iglesia de Santa María la Mayor**. The minaret was converted into a bell tower and a Gothic nave was tacked on to the original structure, followed by a high altar in ornate 16th-century Plateresque style and some finely carved baroque choir stalls. The church overlooks the Plaza de la Duquesa de Parcent, the main square, with the long, elegant façade of the **Ayuntamiento** (Town Hall) gracing another side.

Heading back towards the Puente Nuevo, stop to view the exterior of the **Palacio del Marqués de Salvatierra**, an 18th-century Renaissance mansion famous for its wrought-iron balconies made in traditional Ronda style. Note also the carved stone figures above the entrance.

Nearby stands **La Casa del Rey Moro** (The Moorish King's House), where you will find the remnants of a 14th-century water mine, and gardens designed by the French landscaper Jean Claude Nicolas Foresti-

Ronda perches precariously above the mighty Tajo Gorge

er in the 1920s. A flight of over 300 steps cut out of the rock in Moorish times leads down from the garden to a spring in the gorge. The house does not open its doors to the public, although the gardens do (open daily 10am–7pm).

Beyond here the road curves down towards the Tajo, where two more bridges – the **Puente Viejo** (Old Bridge) built in 1616 on top of Roman foundations and the Moorish **Puente Arabe** – span the gorge and offer striking views of the chasm. Down by the river stands the **Baños Árabes** (Moorish Baths), with the vaulted roof still intact.

Immediately back across the Puente Nuevo, a *parador (see page 106)* occupies what was the old Town Hall and just

Ronda's 18th-century bullring is one of the oldest in all Spain

beyond that is Ronda's neoclassical **Plaza de Toros**, one of the oldest bullrings in Spain. Inaugurated in 1785, it is regarded as the birthplace of the modern bullfight and is something of a shrine to aficionados of the *corrida*. It has a small, but very interesting, museum below the arcaded arena.

Cádiz

The ancient city of **Cádiz**, sitting at the end of a very narrow peninsula of land that runs parallel to the coast, was founded by the Phoenicians in 1100BC and is considered to be Spain's oldest town. In fact, Cádiz's amazing amalgam of history is not readily apparent, with only the remains of the old Roman Theatre to give much evidence of the city's age. It was reconquered by Alfonso X in 1262 and granted the monopoly of trade with Africa by the Catholic Monarchs in 1493. Columbus also departed from this city on his second and fourth voyages in 1493 and 1502 respectively. In the latter part of the 16th century, it twice came under attack by enemy naval forces and a period of prosperity ensued when the Casa de Contratación, the monopoly rights for trade with the Americas, was transferred from Sevilla by order of Felipe V in 1717. A century later, on 19 March 1812, while under attack from Napoleon's forces, the national parliament met in the church of San Felipe Neri and proclaimed the first Spanish parliament.

Of most interest in the town today is the architecturally contrasting baroque and classical **Catedral**, which was constructed between 1772 and 1838. The elegant **Hospital de Mujeres** (Women's Hospital), built even earlier, in 1749, is notable for its patio and art collection, including a fine El Greco. The unusual **Oratorio de la Santa Cueva** church has original underground chapels dating from 1783. Of more interest is the domed upper chapel, which was added in 1796, whose ceiling is adorned by five spectacular paintings – three of which are fine examples of Goya's work. The church of **San Felipe Neri**, mentioned above, is also well worth a look. Built in 1679, it has towering columns and an unusual elliptical dome.

El Puerto de Santa María

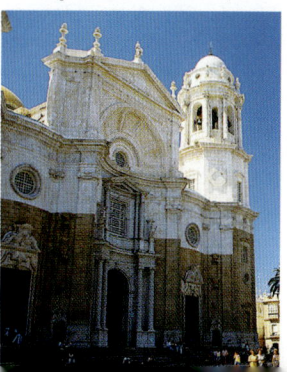

The façade of the Catedral, Cádiz

This small town, on the coast of the Bay of Cádiz, looks across to Cádiz and has considerable charm. It is generally overlooked by foreign visitors, but the Spanish flock here in their thousands, especially during August when there are a series of bullfights. At that time, the

seafood and shellfish restaurants for which El Puerto is famous, are full to overflowing until the early hours. In fact, there isn't too much to see here, but that's okay – El Puerto de Santa María is one of those places that is to be savoured for its ambience. Positioned between Jerez de la Frontera and Cádiz, El Puerto is easily reached by road or rail. However, the most delightful way to get here is on the small ferry, *El Adriano,* which plies its way between the centre of Cádiz and the dockside in El Puerto.

The beach in Puerto de Santa María is popular with Spaniards

Jerez de la Frontera

The name **Jerez de la Frontera** is indicative of two things. It once lay close to the frontier of the old Moorish kingdom of Granada, hence *de la Frontera.* And *Jerez* (pronounced khay-*reth*) gave its name to the wine that has made the town famous, better known to the world in its anglicised version – sherry.

Although known as long ago as the Phoenician era, Jerez first came to prominence under the Moors in the 11th–12th centuries, and it is from that period that the impressively walled and towered **Alcázar** dates. Inside is a simple but elegant mosque that was later converted into a chapel dedicated to Santa María la Real. Reconquered by King Alfonso X in 1264, it became one of the most prosperous towns in Andalucía after the discovery of the Americas and the unification of Spain in 1492. Below the Alcázar is the **Colegiata** (Collegiate Church), a towering dark stone building dating from the 17th and 18th centuries. Housed within is the image of *Cristo de la Viña* (Christ of the Vineyard).

Most *bodegas* in Jerez organise guided tours on weekdays. The visits include a full explanation of the cultivation methods and the production process. In the grounds of the González Byass bodega is a small chamber constructed out of steel by Gustav Eiffel, designer of the eponymous Tower.

It was the development of the sherry wine and brandy business that brought the city worldwide acclaim and more prosperity. It is impossible to walk the streets without recognising *bodegas* (wineries) of prestigious old firms such as Harvey, Williams & Humbert, Gonzalez-Byass and Pedro Domecq. As some of the names imply, it was a group of English merchants who launched Jerez as the world capital of fortified wine. Three centuries on, their descendants continue to control the sherry trade.

Jerez is also famous for its horses. The sherry-producing aristocracy built vast ranches alongside the vineyards, which provided an ideal environment for horse breeding. The Domecq family established the world-famous **Real Escuela Andaluza del Arte Ecuestre** (Spanish Riding School; open Mon–Fri 11am–1pm) in 1973 as a showcase for Andalucían

Sample sherry at the source

**Equestrian expertise in the
Spanish Riding School, Jerez**

equestrian skills. Dressage exhibitions are held on Thursday, but visitors can watch practice sessions on other mornings. The colourful Feria del Caballo (Horse Fair) takes place each May.

Jerez has more subtle attractions, too. In addition to churches and mansions, there's the Centre Andaluza de Flamenco in the Palacio Pemartín and the Museo de Relojes (Clock Museum; open Mon–Sat 10am–1pm) in its own delightful gardens.

Sevilla

The capital of Andalucía, Sevilla is the most Spanish of Spanish cities. It is also one of the most beautiful cities in the world, with a sensual, spiritual and romantic ambience.

It was already a thriving riverside settlement when Julius Caesar arrived in 45BC and under the Romans it developed into a major town. Two Roman emperors, Hadrian and Trajan, were born in nearby Itálica. Subsequently, Sevilla became the capital of the Visigothic kingdom and then of a Moorish *taifa*, before falling to Ferdinand III in 1248. A monopoly of trade with the New World brought the city to its peak during the Golden Age. 'Madrid is the capital of Spain,' the saying went, 'but Sevilla is the capital of the world.'

The two most prominent monuments in the city are around the Plaza del Triunfo. Work on the **Catedral** (open Mon–Sat 11am–5pm, Sun 2–6pm) began in 1401 after the great mosque was razed. The new building followed the ground plan of the old mosque, which accounts for its unusually broad, rectangular form. It is the third largest Christian church in Europe – only St Peter's in Rome and St Paul's in London are bigger.

Massive without, and richly decorated within, the cathedral contains over 30 chapels, including the central **Capilla Mayor** with its Flemish altarpiece and the **Capilla Real** (Royal Chapel), the last resting place of Ferdinand III, the 'King-Saint' who delivered Sevilla from the hands of the infidel. The silver-gilt key to the city, presented to Ferdinand by the vanquished Moors, can be seen in the treasury, along with a cross made from the first gold brought back from the New World by Columbus. The Great Navigator himself is interred nearby, in the huge, ornate 19th-century sarcophagus by the south entrance. His remains were transferred to Sevilla from Havana in 1898, when Cuba won its independence from Spain.

The massive 15th-century Catedral, built on the site of a mosque

To celebrate the recapture of Sevilla by the Christians in 1248, Ferdinand III of Castile rode his horse to the top of the Giralda.

On the north side of the cathedral lies the **Patio de los Naranjos** (Court of the Orange Trees), the ceremonial courtyard of the old mosque with its original ablutions fountains. The minaret, dating from 1184, was preserved as the bell tower of the cathedral *(see photograph on page 18)*. This celebrated tower, **La Giralda** (open Mon–Sat 10.30am–5pm, Sun 2–6pm), is Sevilla's most famous landmark. The exterior is beautifully decorated with typical *sebka* design work which contrasts vividly with the bland interior, where a series of 35 gently elevating ramps lead to an observation platform at a height of 70m (230ft) above the ground.

This is the finest *mirador* in Sevilla and provides stunning views of the old city below. It is surprising to note just how large the Plaza de Toros is when seen from this angle. Look up and you will see how the tower came by its name. In 1356 an earthquake destroyed the original ornamental top and it wasn't until 1558 that the height was raised to 98m (322ft) by the addition of the huge bells and a weather-

The Puerta de León, the main entrance to the Real Alcázar

vane (*giralda* in Spanish) in the form of a statue of a beautiful goddess representing Faith.

The **Real Alcázar** (open Tues–Sat 9.30am–5pm; till 7pm in summer; Sun 9.30am–1.30pm) is a major monument to mid-14th century Mudéjar architecture, combining Moorish, Gothic and Renaissance elements. Built by Moorish craftsmen under Christian rule, during

A graceful Mudéjar archway in the Real Alcázar

the reign of Pedro the Cruel, the rambling palace and its several courtyards incorporate fragments of an earlier Moorish fortress and blend Christian motifs with Moorish designs. You enter on the far side of the square, through the Puerta del León and a visit begins with a tour of the Cuarto del Almirante, where a painting of the Virgen de los Mareantes (Virgin of the Mariners) in the chapel shows Columbus sheltered beneath the Virgin's cloak. The most interesting part is the Patio de las Doncellas (Courtyard of the Maidens), where the rooms preserve outstanding decorative features – ornamental tiles, carved stucco and characteristic coffered *artesonado* ceilings.

The ornate, domed **Salón de Embajadores** (Hall of the Ambassadors) is equal to anything in the Alhambra. Next door is the glass-roofed Patio de las Muñecas (Courtyard of the Dolls), so named for the two tiny human faces carved into the decoration surrounding one of the Moorish arches. These are most unusual, as Muslim craftsmen were forbidden by their religion to depict the human form in their art.

Returning to the entrance courtyard, take the narrow passage on the right to the Patio de Maria Padilla, which sits on

The 13th-century Torre del Oro

top of underground baths. The apartments beyond are hung with Flemish tapestries recording Charles V's Tunis Expedition of 1535, one of them showing an upside-down map of the Mediterranean. Not to be missed, either, are the extensive and beautiful gardens, an oasis of tranquillity in this perpetually busy city.

Nestled around the walls of the Alcazar is the **Barrio de Santa Cruz**, the old Jewish quarter, a picturesque maze of narrow lanes with whitewashed houses and tiny shaded patios that invite leisurely exploration. Just south of the cathedral stands the former exchange building, Casa Lonja, which is now the **Archivo de Indias**. The unusual Cuban wooden shelves are of interest as well as the documents relating to the discovery and conquest of the Americas that rest on them.

Nearby, on the banks of the river, is another of Sevilla's icons. The **Torre del Oro** (Tower of Gold; open Tues–Fri 10am–2pm, Sat–Sun 11am–2pm) is named after the gold-coloured tiles that once covered the walls of this early 13th-century castle. It is all that remains of Sevilla's medieval fortifications and in times of possible invasion a huge metal chain was stretched between here and the other river bank to protect the harbour. Originally used to store treasures brought from the Americas, it was also used as a prison and is now a maritime museum. The round top and spire were added in the middle of the 18th century. A visit to the **Museo de Bellas Artes** (Museum of Fine Arts; open Tues 3–8pm, Wed–Sat 9am–8pm, Sun 9am–2pm), housed in a 17th-century convent, will remind visitors that Sevilla is the birthplace of two of Spain's greatest artists, Velázquez and Murillo.

There are, of course, far too many other places of interest to mention here, but those with a little extra time should visit the **Hospital de la Caridad** (Charity Hospital), the **Museo Taurino** (Bullfighting Museum; open Mon–Sat 10am–1.30pm) and **Plaza de Toros**, the **Parque de los Descubrimientos** (Discovery Park) on the site of Expo '92, and the pedestrian shopping district centred on the **Calle de las Sierpes**. Two of Europe's best-known festivals take place in Sevilla each spring, the **Semana Santa** (Holy Week) parades and the **Fería de Abril** celebration.

Carmona

Carmona, 20km (12 miles) east of Sevilla on the road to Córdoba, sits like a beacon on top of the only hill on an otherwise unrelenting plain. That position has given it strategic importance during its 5,000-year history. It was the Roman era, though, that brought the area prosperity and wealth, and the **Museo y Necropolis** (open Tues–Sat 9am–2pm, 4–6pm, Sun 10am–2pm) is the largest Roman necropolis outside of Rome.

The town's fortunes went into decline after the Romans left, but the Moorish invasion of 713 brought renewed growth and prosperity. The Moors' reign ended in 1247

Carmona's history is unusual because the town was never under feudal rule, but was protected as a satellite of the crown. That is why it is endowed with such an extraordinary number of palaces, mansions, convents and churches.

The fortified Puerta de Sevilla in Carmona's city wall

when Carmona was reconquered by King Ferdinand II. The town was divided among the victors, principally the orders of Santiago and Calatrava. The 14th and 15th centuries were troublesome times as well. The discord was only brought to an end when, in 1630, Felipe IV agreed to grant Carmona the rights of township. The two gates that linked the old Roman road, the **Puerta de Sevilla** and **Puerta de Cordoba**, shouldn't be missed. The Sevilla gate is especially interesting: it is an unusually shaped small fortress.

Córdoba

These days, Córdoba, a minor provincial city sandwiched between Sevilla and Granada, is often passed over by visitors to Andalucía. But to do so is a considerable mistake. Besides being a very agreeable city, it has fabulous historic connections and an eclectic array of attractions to match. Córdoba was once the largest city in Roman Spain, the capital of the province of Batik and the birthplace of Seneca the Younger, philosopher and tragedian. Its golden era was between the mid-8th and very early 11th centuries, when it was the centre of the great medieval caliphate of Córdoba and one of the world's largest and most cultured cities.

The city is dominated by the greatest surviving monument from that period, the Great Mosque, known as **La Mezquita** (open Tues–Sat 10am–7pm, Sun 2–7pm; 5pm in winter) which has the distinction of being the oldest monument in day-to-day use in the Western world. Construction was begun in 786, but it was enlarged three times before attaining its present size in 987. It covers an area of 2 hectares (5 acres). Córdoba was reconquered in 1236 and two small Christian chapels were added in 1258 and 1260. No further major changes were made until the early 16th century when Carlos V decided to construct a Christian cathedral in the centre of the mosque.

Several gateways provide access through the high wall surrounding La Mezquita, the most impressive being the monumental Mudéjar **Puerta del Perdón** (Gate of Forgiveness). Pass through it into the ceremonial forecourt of the **Patio de los Naranjos**, with its fountains and orange trees, to reach the entrance to the mosque. Inside, as your eyes adjust to the dim light, you will see mesmerising rows of columns extending into the shadows in every direction. Antique shafts of porphyry, onyx, marble and jasper, they seem to grow out of the paving stones like trees in an enchanted forest. The double arches overhead, striped in red and white, form a fanciful canopy of curving branches.

At the far end, set in the southeast wall, is the splendid

The magnificent pillared interior of La Mezquita

10th-century **mihrab**, lined with marble and gold mosaics, and the **maksourah**, the enclosure where the caliph attended to his prayers. In the central area of the mosque, restorers have exposed to view a section of the original carved and painted wooden ceiling, which was covered over with vaulting in the 18th century.

The **Catedral**, found at the very centre of the forest of pillars, presents an overpowering contrast to its immediate surroundings. The understated simplicity of Islamic design – and lack of human images – fades completely and is replaced with an ornate blaze of colour within which human images in either paint, stone, or wood abound. Around the walls more Christian chapels line the perimeter of the mosque.

Jardines de los Alcázares

North of La Mezquita lies the labyrinth of narrow streets that makes up the **Barrio de la Judería** (Jewish Quarter). Some of the best restaurants and *tapas* bars in Córdoba are here. Sights to look for include the Callejón de las Flores (Alley of the Flowers), lined with houses built around flower-filled patios that are typical of Córdoba, and the 14th-century **Sinagoga** (open Tues–Sat 10am–2pm, 3.30–5.30pm, Sun 10am–1.30pm) in Calle Judíos. It's a modest affair, just one small room, with a balcony for female worshippers. Córdoba's Jews helped the Moors to gain control of the city in 711 and they lived in peace under the caliphate.

The most illustrious resident of the neighbourhood was Moses Maimónides and a statue of the 12th-century philosopher and theologian stands a few steps from the synagogue in the square named in his honour, **Plaza de Maimónides**. Also here is the **Casa de las Bulas**, which contains El Zoco, a small market of Córdoban craftspeople selling silver filigree and tooled leather goods; and the **Museo Taurino** (open Tues–Sat 9.30am–1.30pm, 5–8pm; Sun 10am–1.30pm).

Northeast of the mosque on the Plaza Jerónimo Paéz, the splendid Renaissance Palacio Paéz houses the **Museo Arqueológico de Córdoba** (open Tues 3–8pm, Wed–Sat 9am–8pm, Sun 9am–3pm). Exhibits span the centuries from the Iberian to the Visigothic period, but pride of place goes to objects from the palace of Medina Azahara, such as the bronze figure of a stag taken from a fountain presented by the Byzantine emperor Constantine VII.

> In its golden age, Córdoba was home to half a million people – almost double today's population. It had the first university and street lighting in Europe, and a library containing more than 400,000 volumes.

A Christian king, Alfonso XI, built Córdoba's **Alcázar de los Reyes Cristianos**, overlooking the river to the southwest of the mosque. The ramparts offer a fine view over the old town and the river, the islets in midstream each occupied by a ruined Moorish mill and the ridges of the Sierra de Córdoba low on the northern horizon. The Catholic Monarchs received Columbus and planned the invasion of Granada while resident here.

Other places that are worth a visit are the 16th-century **Palacio de los Marqueses de Viana**, with its 13 patios, and the 17th-century **Plaza de la Corredera**, the only Castilian-

The colt that gives the Plaza del Potro its name

style plaza in Andalucía. Stroll to the unusual **Plaza del Potro**, which gets its name (Square of the Colt) from the fountain in the centre, dating from 1577. The square is home to two interesting museums: the **Museo de Bellas Artes** (Fine Arts Museum; open Tues 3–8pm, Wed–Sat 9am–8pm, Sun 9am–3pm; reduced opening times in winter) and the ever-popular **Julio Romero de Torres Museum** (open Tues–Sat 10am–2pm, 6–8pm, Sun 9.30am–3pm; reduced opening times in winter) a museum devoted to the Córdoban artist of the same name. He was born nearby and specialised in mildly erotic paintings of beautiful Córdoban women.

Eight kilometres (5 miles) west of Córdoba lie the ruins of the intriguing **Medina Azahara** (Madinat al-Zahra). It was commissioned in 936 by Abd-ar-Rahman III in honour of his favourite concubine, Al Zahra (The Flower). Detailed records indicate that building materials for the grand design were brought from Constantinople and various North African locations. Despite such auspicious beginnings, it had a short life; the palace was razed with the break-up of the caliphate of Córdoba in the early 11th century. Many of the materials were subsequently used on constructions in Sevilla and elsewhere. For nearly 900 years, it was left in ruins and not until 1910 did the slow work of excavation begin. This still continues, but reconstructed royal apartments give some impression of the magnificence of this sumptuous complex of baths, schools, gardens and stately apartments, built on three terraces.

Alcalá la Real

The road from Córdoba to Granada is, in many sections, rather dramatic; you pass through mountainous scenery and olive groves (Jaén Province is the largest olive-growing area in the world), dotted with little white-walled towns often crowned with castles. The last sizeable town before Granada, **Alcalá la Real**, was a Moorish fortified city from the early 8th century and remained a strategic bastion until the reconquest of Granada in 1492, after which further Christian monuments were added. The **Fortaleza de la Mota**, on the summit at 1,033m (3,389ft), is an amazing complex combining Moorish and Christian influences, along with spectacular views. A particular fascination, and one that is both beautiful and gruesome, is the semi-ruined church whose floor has been partly excavated, leaving tombs with bones and skulls exposed.

The splendid Medina Azahara survived for less than a century

The mighty Alhambra towers over Granada

Granada

The Nasrid dynasty rose to power in Granada just as the fortunes of the Spanish Moors were beginning to wane *(see page 17)*. The first of the line, Mohammed ben Alhamar, established his capital here in 1232, after Ferdinand III had forced him from Jaén. Two years later, Moors fleeing from the newly vanquished Sevilla swelled the population, which had already been augmented by refugees from Córdoba. Rather than grieve for the homes they had left behind, the industrious Moors set about making Granada the grandest city of Al Andalus. Over the course of the next century, the hilltop palace of the Alhambra took shape. Granada was the last of the great Moorish kingdoms of Andalucía to be reconquered, and King Boabdil's surrender to the Catholic Monarchs in January 1492 marked the end of the Muslim Empire in Spain.

The second most visited monument in Spain is the world-famous **Alhambra** (open daily; advance booking strongly recommended; tel: 902 224 460; combined ticket with Alcazaba and the Palacio Generalife). It takes its name, which means 'the red one', from the red-brown bricks used in the construction of its outer walls, which rise precipitously above the deep gorge of the Río Darro. Its strategically placed towers command superb views over the city below.

Within the walls of the Alhambra, there are four main areas to explore, which are best taken in the following order: the **Alcazaba** (fortress), the **Casa Real Vieja** (Old Royal Palace), the **Casa Real Nueva** (New Royal Palace) and finally the **Generalife** (summer gardens). Amazingly, this complex was allowed to fall into almost total disrepair over the centuries and was used as a barracks for Napoleon's troops during the Wars of Independence. It wasn't until 1870 that it was designated a National Monument.

The Alcazaba is the oldest part of the Alhambra and only the impressive outer walls and towers survive. The main attraction is the view from the Torre de la Vela, north over Albaicín and Sacramonte and south to the high snow-capped peaks of the Sierra Nevada.

The highlight of the monument is the Palacio Nazaríes, the magnificent home of the rulers of the kingdom of Granada. It is actually a series of palaces, each with its own patios, fountains

Washington Irving

Irving was an American writer who is best known for *The Sketch Book*, a collection of stories that included such classics as *The Legend of Sleepy Hollow* and *Rip Van Winkle*. From 1826 until 1832, he was attached to the American legation in Spain, where he became fascinated by the legends of Moorish Andalucía. During his stay in Granada, he moved into the apartments of Carlos V while writing *Tales of the Alhambra*, a collection of stories about Granada's Moorish past.

The exquisite Patio de Arrayanes

and other adornments. The intricacy, delicacy and sheer beauty of the design creates a visual impression that is beyond mere words.

The **Salón de Embajadores** (Hall of the Ambassadors), or royal audience chamber, is one of the most ornate rooms in the Alhambra. Skirted with geometric tiling, the walls and roof are overlaid with delicately shaped plaster stalactites, reaching 18m (60ft) to the carved and painted wooden ceiling. Verses from the Koran and the name of the 14th-century monarch Yusuf I are woven into the design. Through the tall, arched windows are magnificent views of Albaicín and the Darro. The **Sala de los Abencerrajes** recalls the aristocratic family of that name, that was accused of disloyalty and collusion with the Christians by Boabdil. The king invited the Abencerrajes to a reception in this room and massacred all 36 of the unsuspecting family members. Also of particular interest are the **Patio de los Leones**, whose name derives from the splashing fountain in the centre upheld by 12 stone lions, the **Torre de las Damas** (Tower of the Ladies) and the old bath area.

The Casa Real Nueva, though imposing, is, as the name implies, relatively new and architecturally at odds with the more ornate older palaces, some of which were destroyed to make way for it. Commissioned by Carlos V in 1527, its exterior is in the shape of a square, with a surprisingly elegant two-storey circular patio on the inside. Considered on its own merits, the building must be regarded as a fine example of Renaissance architecture.

Two museums are housed inside the palace. The first, the **Museo Nacional de Arte Hispano-Musulmán** (Museum of Hispano-Moorish Art;

> In 1494, only two years after the Alhambra had been captured by Christian forces, the German historian, Hieronymus Münzer wrote: 'There is nothing like it in Europe; it is so magnificent, so majestic, so exquisitely fashioned... that one cannot be sure one is not in Paradise.'

open Tues–Sat 9am–2.30pm), displays such evocative artefacts as the throne of the Nasrids, a wooden armchair inlaid with silver and ivory, and the Alhambra Vase, which once graced the Hall of the Two Sisters. The second, the **Museo de Bellas Artes** (Fine Arts Museum; open Tues–Sat 10am–2pm), contains a collection of works chronicling the development of the school of Granada between the 16th and 19th centuries.

The Generalife is found at the eastern end of the Alhambra fortifications on the neighbouring hillside. A modest summer palace, it is surrounded by beautiful terraced gardens where oleander and roses bloom luxuriantly and delicate fountains and cascades play among the neatly clipped cypress hedges.

Back down in the city, the most prominent monument is the exquisite **Capilla Real** (Royal Chapel), a Renaissance chapel that serves as the mausoleum of the Catholic Monarchs. The effigies of Ferdinand and Isabella lie on the right-hand side of the chancel, with those of their daughter Juana La Loca and her husband Felipe El Hermoso on the slightly higher monument on the left. Their mortal remains have been interred in the crypt underneath since 1521, after being ceremonially transferred from the Alhambra. On exhibition in the **sacristy** are mementos of the Catholic Monarchs, including Ferdinand's sword and Isabella's sceptre and crown, a circle of gold embellished with acanthus scrolls.

The **Catedral** (open daily 10.30am–1pm, 4–7.30pm) next door is large and imposing. A few steps away is the **Alcaicería** area, the old silk market of the Moors. These days, it's a colourful collection of narrow lanes with a concentration of outlets for handicrafts and souvenirs. Not far away is the **Corral del Carbón** (House of Coal). Dating from the 12th century, it is the oldest Moorish monument in the city and is now a centre for typical Granadino arts and crafts.

Albaicín, the old Moorish district on the hill opposite the Alhambra, has a maze of narrow streets and staircases surrounding its ancient whitewashed houses and enclosed patio gardens. Down by the Río Darro is the exquisite **Casa de Castril**, dating from 1539 and home of the Archaeological Museum, and the nearby 11th-century **El Bañuelo** (Moorish Baths). Further up the hill is the **Mirador San Nicolás**. From here, you get the best view of the Alhambra, with the snow-capped Sierra Nevada in the background – a scene replicated on countless postcards.

High up to the right of Albaicín is the *Gitano* (Gypsy) area of Sacramonte, famous for its caves and *tablaos* (literally, stages) where gypsies, for the benefit of tourists, re-enact wedding ceremonies. Tourists should be wary, especially at night, as this is not the safest part of town.

Guadix

About 50km (32 miles) east of Granada on the road to Murcia is **Guadix**, a particularly unusual city in that many of its inhabitants are troglodytes. In the Barrio Santiago are streets of houses with small front yards that are indistinguishable from ordinary homes. Look closely, though, and the white, circular chimneys emanating from the rocks give the game away. These are actually caves with a practical use: they're cool in summer and warm in winter. There is plenty more of interest here, including a Moorish castle dating from the 10th and 11th centuries, a late 16th-century cathedral and many important palaces, houses and churches.

The whitewashed chimneys of the cave-dwellings of Guadix

Las Alpujarras

This is a remote area even today, located as it is between the Sierra Nevada and Sierra de la Contraviesa mountain ranges, with the southern slopes of the latter dropping graciously into the Mediterranean. It is dotted with small towns and villages that retain many appearances of a lifestyle long since departed from other areas. The way of life here in the early 20th century was detailed by Gerald Brenan in his book *South from Granada*.

In fact, these communities fall into one of two areas according to their altitude and climate: **La Alpujarra Alta** (the High Alpujarra), just south of the highest peaks in the Sierra Nevada and **La Alpujarra Baja** (the Low Alpujarra) in the Sierra de la Contraviesa. **Trevélez**, the highest village in Spain, is famous for its *jamón serrano* (dried cured ham) and **Lanjarón** is familiar throughout Spain as the name on the red, green and white label on bottles of water originating from the town's springs. Incidentally, that same water runs free from the *fuentes* (fountains) of many villages.

Air-dried hams in Trevélez

The main entrance to Las Alpujarras is from the Granada to Motril road, the same road along which the defeated Moors travelled on their way into exile. Even today, there is a pass 12km (8 miles) south of Granada that bears the sad name **El Suspiro del Moro** (The Sigh of the Moor). It is from here that distant Granada finally fades from view and it is said that the defeated King Boabdil sighed with regret as he looked back at the city. His mother apparently had little sympathy. She is reported to have told him: 'Don't cry like a woman for something you could not defend as a man.'

PROTECTED LANDSCAPES

Andalucía has an abundance of natural parks and wildlife reserves, ranging from those with an international reputation to more obscure, remote nature preserves. These are some of the most interesting ones.

The Sierra Morena. This mountain range runs nearly 480km (300 miles) from the mountains of southern Portugal in the west to the border of the Provincia de Murcia in the east, effectively forming the border between Andalucía and most of the rest of Spain.

Covering an area of 5,240 sq. km (2,023 sq. miles), the Sierra Morena encompasses no fewer than seven natural parks – the Sierra de Aracena y Picos de Aroche; the Sierra Norte de Sevilla; the Sierra de Hornachuelos; the Sierra Cardeña y Montoro; the Sierra de Andújar; Despeñaperros; and the Sierra de Cazorla, Segurla y Las Villas. Each has its own attributes and the whole area is a stronghold of the Spanish lynx, but the highest peaks and the most dramatic scenery are found in the last of these, which is also the birthplace of the great Río Guadalquivir.

El Torcal de Antequera and the **Fuente de Piedra**. Just south of the town of Antequera is one of the more famous geological formations in Spain. The limestone mountains of the El Torcal de Antequera have eroded to form some of the most unusual shapes seen anywhere. In fact, these formations so resemble modern sculptures that they have been assigned comical names. Just north of Antequera, droughts notwithstanding, is the Fuente de Piedra, Andalucía's largest lake, with a surface area that can reach 1,384 hectares (3,420 acres). Each spring, if weather conditions are favourable, the lake becomes a home to flamingos. In fact, it is the only inland breeding area in Europe for this colour-

The Sierra de Cazorla is the biggest nature reserve in Andalucía

ful species, and a good year can see up to 11,000 pairs. In spring, the islet of La Colonia becomes particularly crowded. Over 150 species of birds have been identified on the lake and in the surrounding areas.

Doñana National Park. This is probably the most famous park in Spain. It holds many national and international honours and is listed as a World Heritage Site. Consisting of 862 sq. km (333 sq. miles), it is bordered on one side by the Atlantic Ocean and on another the Río Guadalquivir as it winds down from Sevilla to reach the ocean at Sanlúcar de Barrameda. In fact, Doñana is the last great lowland wilderness sanctuary in southern Europe and has three distinct ecosystems: the *marismas* (salt marshes), the *matorral* (brushwood) and the *dunas* (sand dunes). Within its bounds can be found an amazing array of animal, bird and plant life, but what you see depends on the time of year you visit.

> The most convenient way to see Doñana National Park is on a tour organised by Coop. Andaluz Marismas del Rocio, whose large-wheel buses depart from the visitors' centre at El Acebuche. It's a very bumpy, rough ride and only advisable if you are fit and agile.

Laguna de Medina. Across the Guadalquivir and about 10km (6 miles) east of Jerez de la Frontera is this small lake, one of the last stops in Europe for birds migrating south from northern and central Europe to Africa at the end of August. In periods of drought it is attractive to birds that usually reside at Doñana and around 50 species have been observed here.

Grazalema. A short distance to the east of Laguna de Medina is the mainly mountainous wilderness of the Parque Natural de Grazalema. Its 517 sq. km (200 sq. miles) are home to three species of eagles and numerous other birds, mammals and reptiles. The mountains here, ranging between 1,000 and 1,700m (3,300–5,600ft), are the first stop for clouds arriving from the Atlantic, giving the area the highest rainfall in Spain – and encouraging a fine array of flora. Of particular note is the rare Spanish fir *(Abies pinsapo)*. The little village of Grazalema is extremely pretty and makes a good base for walkers.

Sierra Nevada and Las Alpujarras. This national park, one of the most recently created, has the distinction of having the highest peak on the Spanish mainland (Mulhacén is 3,482m/11,420ft tall), as well as a wide diversity of flora made possible by the nearby Mediterranean Biosphere Reserve. It also has the highest road in Europe. Along it is the Solynieve (literally Sun and Snow) ski resort, accessible all year round at some 2,500m (8,000ft) and the more elevated Pico Veleta (Weathercock Peak) at 3,398m (11,148ft), which can only be reached during a few short weeks in the summer.

The hillsides of Las Alpujarras near Trevélez, Spain's highest village

WHAT TO DO

SPORTS

Most visitors to the Costa del Sol do not plan daytime activities that are any more energetic than lazing on the beach, and save their energy for nightlife. However, sports facilities are there in abundance for those who want to work off the effects of too much paella.

Water Sports

The main resort beaches offer all kinds of sports equipment for hire, as well as beach umbrellas and loungers, and the larger beach restaurants have toilet facilities; some provide changing rooms.

Swimming: With more than 160km (100 miles) of beaches, the Costa del Sol offers plenty of spots for swimming. Most of the sandy strands lie to the west of Málaga, while shingle and rocks (with some sandy coves) predominate to the east. In the high season, the most popular beaches are mobbed. You stand the best chance of finding a patch of sand to yourself to the east of Nerja and west of Estepona. Many beaches now fly the blue flag, which means that water quality and general sanitation meets the EU's environmental standards.

Boating: There are numerous marinas along the coast between Málaga and Sotogrande, providing year-round moorings for yachts and motor boats. Some offer boats for day rentals and longer-term charters (with or without skipper and crew). Marbella has three such establishments and many of the beaches and larger beach hotels hire sailing boats.

Waterskiing: The main resorts all have waterskiing schools, and most big hotels offer instruction. Prices are generally

Windsurfers travel to Tarifa from all round the world

high, but they vary. Swimming and skiing areas often overlap.

Windsurfing: This sport is the coast's fastest-growing activity, with boards, sails and professional instruction available in most of the resort areas. The season runs from March to November with strongest winds in June and September.

Snorkelling and Scuba Diving: Snorkelling can be an engrossing activity, particularly off the rocky, indented stretch of coast beyond Nerja. If you dive or snorkel any distance from shore, you are legally required to tow a marker buoy. Diving centres operate in several resorts. For more information, contact the local tourist office *(see page 128)*.

Angling: Fishing from the rocks and breakwaters is a popular pastime with local people and no permit is required. The deeper waters offshore teem with tunny (tuna), swordfish and shark. Deep-sea fishing boats can be hired at the marinas and many resort hotels make arrangements for fishing expeditions. A very popular inland fishing spot is the Pantanos del Chorro (*pantano* means reservoir) at the Chorro Dam *(see page 31)*. Freshwater anglers must have a permit – ask at the nearest tourist office for information on how to obtain one.

Fishing from a breakwater

Other Sports

Golf: When it comes to variety, few resort areas in the world can compare with the Costa del Sol. There are some 30 18-hole courses between Málaga and Gibraltar. Most private and hotel clubs welcome non-residents or non-members, though some may charge visitors a higher fee. Clubs, caddies and carts are generally available for hire.

The quality of the courses is excellent – many have been designed by such famous names as Robert Trent Jones and Seve Ballesteros. Las Brisas, near Marbella, has staged the Spanish Open and Valderrama, near Sotogrande, was host to the 1997 Ryder Cup. Although a private club, Valderrama has nine starting times between midday and 2pm that are open to the public, albeit at around €200 per round. For details of golf courses and fees, consult the monthly magazine *Costa Golf*, an English-language publication.

Cycling through the Sierra de Cazorla

Tennis and Squash: Some of the biggest names in tennis are linked to the numerous clubs, centres and 'ranches' on the Costa del Sol, including the Marbella-based Manolo Santana Tennis Club, which hosts the majority of Spain's Davis Cup matches and other important tournaments.

Cycling: Bikes can be hired at towns up and down the coast and inland (where mountain roads and trails are ideal for mountain-biking).

Hiking: There are a number of good hiking areas within easy reach of the coast, notably the Parque Nacional Montes de Málaga just north of Málaga and El Torcal de Antequera and La Garganta del Chorro a little further inland *(see page 30)*.

For more good walks, try the area around Ronda, and the hills above the Refugio de Juanar near Marbella *(see page 40)*.

Horse Riding: Andalucía is famous for both horses and horsemanship. There are stables on the coast and near the inland cities, with mounts for hire; you can canter along the open beach or ride up into the hills.

Skiing: Few people think of the Costa del Sol as a ski resort, but skiing can be enjoyed between December and May at the Solynieve resort near Granada, 160km (100 miles) northeast of Málaga in the Sierra Nevada. Situated near the summit of Mt Veleta, it is Europe's southernmost ski resort.

SHOPPING

Most shops are open from 9.30 or 10am–1.30 or 2pm and from 4.30–8pm. The siesta *(see below)* is still religiously observed in southern Spain. But in summer, shops in the tourist resorts stay open throughout the day until 8.30pm or later. Department stores and supermarkets do not close for the siesta.

> The siesta is an afternoon nap taken to avoid the hottest part of the day. It means that many shops and businesses take a three-hour lunch break, closing from 1 or 2pm till 4 or 5pm, and then opening up again until 7.30pm. This age-old custom seems to be dying out in some parts of northern Spain, but it is still observed in Andalucía.

Markets

Weekly open-air markets are held on Monday in Marbella, Tuesday in Nerja and Fuengirola, Wednesday in Estepona, Thursday in Torremolinos and San Pedro de Alcántara, and Friday in Benalmádena. Most cities have a *rastro* (flea market) on Sunday morning. Of these, Sevilla's is the largest and the town also has a coin-and-stamp and small animal market on the same day.

Shopping for souvenirs in the Alcaicería district in Granada

Where to Shop

The larger cities offer lower prices and a better selection of goods than resorts like Torremolinos or Fuengirola. The El Corte Inglés department store, with branches in Málaga, Sevilla and other places, is also well worth looking for.

For more sophisticated shopping, nothing can compare with Marbella or Puerto Banús, where dozens of attractive harbour-front boutiques offer a stunning selection of merchandise at equally stunning prices.

You can make a considerable saving on luxury goods like jewellery, watches, perfumes and Havana cigars in duty-free Gibraltar, where there is no VAT (called IVA in Spain).

Ceuta, the Spanish protectorate on the North African coast, has special tax status. Alcohol, for example, is vastly cheaper there than in mainland Spain. The same applies to electrical goods, but while the prices may seem very reasonable to northern European visitors, they will not be much of a bargain for Americans.

Pottery from Purullena

What to Buy

Traditional Spanish handicrafts are high on any souvenir-hunter's shopping list.

Ceramics: Everyday glazed terracotta pottery can be bought all along the coast. There is also a wide selection of tiles *(azulejos)*, vases, bowls and jugs, with floral or geometric decorations in bright colours.

Foodstuffs: Take home a taste of Spain with some olives, olive oil, almonds, cheese or mouthwatering biscuits.

Jewellery: Silver rings, bracelets and necklaces in modern designs make good buys, as do the artificial Majorica pearls of Spain. Look, too, for fine filigree jewellery from Córdoba, and smooth, polished olive-wood beads.

Leather and Suede: Choose from a wide selection of handbags, belts, wallets, trousers, skirts and coats. Leather goods, while no longer the bargain they once were, still compare favourably in price with Italian- and French-made articles, and the local factories turn out stylish, high-quality leather clothing. Córdoba, which has been producing leather goods since Roman times, is famous for its embossed leather. But beware: many of the leather goods you will see for sale have been imported from Morocco and are sold at inflated prices. It's actually cheaper, and much more interesting, to take a day trip to Tangier and buy such goods there.

Souvenirs: Often delightfully tacky, from plastic castanets and flamenco dolls to imitation wineskins and even bullfight posters printed with your own name.

Wine and Spirits: Sweet Málaga wine, sherry, brandy and Spanish wines provide some of the best bargains in Spain, and are generally cheaper when bought in a supermarket than at the airport duty-free shop.

ENTERTAINMENT

Tour operators offer any number of excursions, some more esoteric than others, with brochures and booking facilities available through your hotel or a local travel agent.

Bullfights: Andalucía is famed for its bullfighting traditions, and has two of the seven first-class *Plazas de Toros* (bull-rings) in Spain (in Sevilla and Córdoba). The provincial capitals of Almería, Granada, Huelva, Jaén and Málaga as well as Algeciras and El Puerto de Santa María have second-class rings. All others, including those in the resort towns along the Costa del Sol, fall into the third class. The two main events are a *corrida de toros*, where fully qualified

Matador statue in Ronda

matadors fight fully-grown *toros* (bulls), of at least four years old; and *novilladas*, where *novilleros* (novice matadors) fight *novillos* (immature bulls).

As a rule of thumb, the better events are held in the better plazas, particularly during the *ferías* (fairs) in the major cities. Equally true is the fact that most of the events held in the resort towns are mainly for the benefit of tourists and are of lesser quality – although they are not generally less expensive. Smaller rings mean fewer seats, which often equates to higher prices. Outside of the *ferías* – when they are held daily – only Sevilla has bullfights on a regular basis. In other places, with the exception of Easter Sunday and 15 August – important national holidays – they are held sporadically and advertised by way of the ubiquitous *carteles* (posters) stuck on every wall. The perceived cruelty of bullfights arouses very strong feelings among Americans and northern Europeans. They are, however, very much part of the southern Spanish culture.

Flamenco: All the coastal resorts offer flamenco shows for tourists. They can be highly entertaining, but they are more in the spirit of show business than true flamenco. To experience flamenco at its most authentic, you will have to search out

The Sound of Andalucía

Flamenco is an ancient art form, combining elements of Visigothic, Moorish and gypsy music. There are two distinct types; the *cante jondo* (deep song), an intense outpouring of emotion; and the animated *cante chico* (light song). There are also different varieties of flamenco dance, including the *tango*, *fandango*, *farruca* and *zambra*), performed to the staccato rhythms and counter-rhythms of the castanets, hand clapping *(palmadas)* and finger snapping *(pitos)*, as well as furious heel-drumming *(zapateado)*. There is no need to speak Spanish to enjoy the spectacle – you simply have to feel the music.

bars and small clubs in Málaga, Granada or Sevilla. Ask the local tourist office for advice on where to go.

Discos and Nightclubs: Some discos open as early as 9pm, but most don't gear up for business until 11pm or midnight. They close late, too, around 4am or even later. Nightclubs *(salas de fiesta)* usually stage two shows an evening, one at about midnight or 1am and the other around 3am. Depending on the club, the show may feature flamenco performances, drag acts, or shows with semi-nude women. Bars, pubs and clubs often provide musical entertainment.

Flamenco performance in Córdoba

Casinos: There are two gambling establishments that operate from 8pm to the early hours: Casino Torrequebrada in Benalmádena-Costa, and Casino Marbella, under the Hotel Andalucía Plaza in Puerto Banús. In addition to the usual games, the casinos have a bar, restaurant and nightclub on the premises. Formal dress (jacket and tie for men) is required. Don't forget to bring your passport for identification.

Concerts: From May to October, Tívoli World brings the stars of rock and pop to Torremolinos for concerts in the open air. The season's programme may include performances of flamenco and *zarzuela* (Spanish light opera). In winter, Málaga's symphony orchestra performs in the Teatro Cervantes theatre, and guest artists appear at Castillo El Bil-Bil in Benalmádena-Costa.

ACTIVITIES FOR CHILDREN

The Costa del Sol is an ideal place for families with kids – it is, after all, one long beach. Apart from paddling and sand-castles, older children can learn how to sail, waterski or wind-surf. If you don't feel happy about letting your children play in the sea, especially the younger ones, the water parks at Mijas, Torremolinos and Estepona offer a safer and more controlled environment where it's easier to keep a close eye on them.

Alternative diversions for children include the **aquariums** in Benalmádena and Puerto Banús, the **Eagle Park** in Benalmá-dena, the Cueva (cave) de Nerja, and **Mini-Hollywood** near Almería. In the evening, **Tívoli World** near Benalmá-dena provides all the fun of the fair, with carnival rides and a roller coaster, and there's also a bar and flamenco show for the grown-ups. **Crocodile Park** just north of Málaga, will intrigue most children, as will the horse shows at **El Ranchito** in Benalmádena and Aires del Sur in Estepona.

Dressed for the fair

On the beach, don't forget that children are especially vulnerable to the sun. Take high-factor sunscreen and sun hats and make sure they are covered up during the middle of the day, and wear T-shirts in the water (a siesta during the hottest part of the day may be a good idea).

Calendar of Events

January: *Cabalgata de Reyes* (Three Kings' Parade), Málaga. On 5 January, the eve of Epiphany, floats, bands and traditionally costumed characters commemorate the visit of the Wise Men to the infant Christ.

March/April: *Semana Santa* (Holy Week), throughout the area. Sombre processions of hooded penitents and religious images every night during the week before Easter. Most impressive in Sevilla, Málaga and Granada.

April: *Feria de Abril* (April Fair, starts 10 days after Easter), Sevilla. Horses and riders, bullfights, flamenco, fireworks and parties in the streets are part of Andalucía's most colourful festival.

April/May: *Feria del Caballo* (Horse Fair), Jerez de la Frontera. Spain's equestrian showcase, with events of all kinds, including racing, dressage and carriage competitions.

May: *Romería de San Isidro* (Pilgrimage of St Isidore), Estepona, Nerja. Decorated carts and costumed riders parade in Estepona, while Nerja stages concerts, folk dancing and fireworks.

June: *Corpus Christi*, throughout the area. Bullfights and fireworks enliven this national holiday, a big event in Granada.

June/July: *Festival Internacional de Música y Danza*, Granada. Concerts and dance performed outdoors in the Alhambra and Generalife.

July: *Virgen del Carmen*, coastal towns. Processions of fishing boats pay tribute to the Virgin of Carmen, protector of fishermen.

August: *Feria de Málaga* (Málaga Fair), Málaga. A carnival, circus, bullfights and flamenco events enliven the first fortnight of the month. *Festival de España*, Nerja. The town's famous cave provides the eerie venue for this subterranean celebration of music and dance.

September: *Feria de Ronda* (Ronda Fair), Ronda. The highlight of this fair is the *corrida goyesca*, a costumed bullfight held in Ronda's 18th-century ring. *Fiesta de la Vendímia* (Wine Harvest Festival), Jerez de la Frontera. A parade, bullfights, flamenco and equestrian events follow the blessing of the grape harvest.

December 28: *Fiesta de Verdiales*, Málaga. Groups from all over the province gather to celebrate this early style of folk song and dance.

EATING OUT

You could easily spend your entire holiday on the Costa del Sol without ever sitting down to a real Spanish meal. In the big coastal resorts the range of eating places is amazing: hamburger stands, pizza bars, pub grub, beach barbecues and restaurants of almost any nationality you can think of, with a few Spanish ones thrown in for good measure. In fact, you could eat bacon and eggs, beans on toast, steak and chips and other standard British fare every day, without going into the same restaurant twice. But for those visitors keen to sample the delights of the local cuisine, there are numerous fine Spanish restaurants on the coast and many, many more throughout Andalucía.

WHERE TO EAT

One of Spain's most civilised institutions is the **tapas** bar, or *tasca*. Originally, the idea was that when you ordered a drink, generally beer or wine only, a small helping of a tasty morsel and a couple of pieces of bread were given free. The food was served on a small plate, traditionally used to cover the glass, and came to be called a *tapa*, which literally means lid. These days, when tapas joints have sprung up throughout the cities of Europe, such authentic bars, with free morsels, are hard to find. There is invariably a charge, which varies depending on what you choose. Although this is still a fine way of sampling a number of different dishes, it can easily become costlier than selecting an inexpensive *menú del día* (set menu).

Cafeterias are middle-range establishments, common in the resorts, usually offering a selection of *platos combinados* (combination dishes), such as a pork chop and chips, or squid and salad, with bread and a drink included.

El Peñon restaurant overlooks the beach in Salobreña

A *comedor*, literally 'dining room', is often a small area at the back of a bar where you can sit down and dig into a basic but satisfying meal. *Comedors* tend, on the whole, to cater to local workers: cheap and cheerful, they are usually open for lunch only.

Restaurantes proper are pretty much the same as anywhere else; they are usually open for lunch and dinner, and close during the afternoon and one day a week. They may offer a *menú del día* which will be much cheaper than ordering à la carte. A restaurant calling itself a *marisquería* specialises in shellfish and seafood, while an *asador* is the place for roast meats. A *venta* is a small, family-run restaurant serving down-to-earth country fare, and is well worth looking out for if you venture away from the coast.

First-time visitors to Spain are often surprised by the late eating hours: the Spanish rarely sit down to lunch *(almuerzo)* before 2pm, and dinner *(cena)* starts around 9.30 or

10pm. However, in the resort areas many restaurants stay open throughout the day.

Although restaurants usually include service in the bill, it is customary to leave an additional tip (about 10 percent).

WHAT TO EAT

Breakfast

The traditional Spanish breakfast generally consists of *churros y chocolate* (doughnut-like fritters and thick, sweet, drinking chocolate) taken standing up at the counter in a café or roadside *kiosko*. Alternatively, try a *tostada con aceite* (toasted roll with olive oil) washed down with *café con leche* (milky coffee). Spanish espresso *(café solo)* is strong stuff, even with a touch of milk *(un cortado)*. Resort hotels often offer a full buffet breakfast and, of course, a full English breakfast isn't hard to find.

Enjoying tapas in Jerez

Tapas

Every good bar offers a selection of tapas. Among the dozens of items to choose from, you may find sweet red peppers in olive oil seasoned with garlic, Russian salad, slices of sausage (both spicy *chorizo* and paprika-flavored *salchichón*), *jamón serrano* (cured ham), marinated mussels, baby squid, clams or *tortilla española* (Spanish omelette, with potato and onion filling, usually served cold in slices). For a larger portion of any given tapa, ask for a *ración*. If you feel that's too much for you, order a *media ración*.

Soups

Andalucía's most famous speciality is the cold soup known as *gazpacho*. There are dozens of ways to make it, but the version you are likely to find in southern Spain is a creamy chilled blend of cucumber, tomato, onion, and crushed garlic, with freshly diced green pepper, tomato and cucumber, chopped hard-boiled egg and fried croutons on the side.

Be sure to try the mixed fish or shellfish soups, *sopa de pescado* and *sopa de mariscos*. Like its French counterpart, the Mediterranean *bouillabaisse*, *sopa marinera* is based on the day's catch and seasoned with tomato, onion, garlic and a dash of white wine or brandy.

Originally from Málaga, *ajo blanco* (white garlic soup) is a variation on the more common *gazpacho* theme. Ground almonds and garlic form the base of this summer refresher, served ice-cold with a garnish of almonds and grapes.

Vegetable Dishes

The Spanish usually eat vegetables as a first course, rather than as an accompanying dish. But whatever you do, don't miss that great speciality of Andalucía, *alcachofas a la Montilla* – artichoke leaves cooked in a mixture of wine and beef broth, thickened with flour and seasoned with mint, garlic and saffron. *Judías verdes con salsa de tomate*, green beans in tomato sauce laced with garlic, can also be very good.

Egg Dishes

Egg dishes make popular starters, and a whole Spanish omelette is a filling lunch on its own. *Tortillas* (omelettes) may be filled with asparagus, tuna or mushrooms. *Huevos a la flamenca* is a baked dish of eggs cooked on a base of tomato, garlic and herbs – usually accompanied by diced ham or spicy *chorizo* sausage, fresh peas and sweet red peppers.

Seafood

The seafood you are served in the waterfront restaurants was probably landed on the beach that very morning by the fishermen whose boats lie hauled up on the sand.

The traditional Torremolinos lunch is sardines skewered on a wooden spike and grilled over a charcoal fire on the beach. This simple but tasty dish is irresistible and extremely good value. Squid may be an interesting option, either cooked in its own ink *(calamares en su tinta)*, a spicy dish, or simply dipped in batter and fried, and served with a twist of lemon. *Gambas* and *cigalas* are large juicy prawns – choose your own from the display and have them grilled while you choose your wine.

When it's available, *langosta* (lobster) is excellent served hot with butter or cold with mayonnaise. *Boquerones* (fresh anchovies) and *chanquetes* (whitebait) are tossed in flour and deep-fried whole. *Merluza*, or hake, may be served fried, boiled or mushroom-stuffed, perhaps with tomatoes and potatoes. *Besugo* (sea bream) is a high-quality fish, brushed with olive oil and simply grilled.

A Torremolinos lunch: fresh sardines grilled over a wood fire

Other common items on the menu may include *pez espada* (swordfish), *mero* (sea bass), *bonito* (tuna) and *rape* (monkfish). If you have difficulty deciding what to try, you may want to plump for the *fritura malagueña*, a mixed fish fry that includes all of the above seafood. Be warned, though, many of these delicacies are priced on the menu for a 100-g (approximately 4-oz) portion, so what appears to be an inexpensive dish will prove very costly when you see the final bill.

Paella

Spain's most famous dish, which the Spaniards usually eat at lunchtime, deserves to be discussed separately. The main ingredient of paella is

Paellas of many kinds, served alongside burgers and beans

saffron-flavoured rice, cooked with olive oil, seafood and chicken. But every cook has his or her own variation on this colourful dish that originated in Valencia on Spain's eastern coast. The name paella derives from the flat, round metal pan in which it is cooked.

The secret of perfect paella is fresh ingredients; fresh seafood such as *langosta* (spiny lobster), *langostinos* (a kind of large shrimp), *cigalas* (giant prawns or sea crayfish), *gambas* (prawns), mussels, together with chicken, peas, sweet peppers and artichoke hearts, all cooked together slowly as the rice absorbs the juices. It also comes with a meat base, perhaps involving rabbit or pork as well as chicken.

Chicken and Meat

Spanish chicken is delicious, whether fried, roasted or braised in white wine or sherry with almonds. The staple *arroz con pollo* (chicken with rice) is tasty.

Many traditional meat dishes make use of offal such as tripe, brains and sweetbreads. *Riñones al Jerez*, kidneys sautéed with sherry, or *rabo de toro*, braised oxtail served in a rich tomato sauce with carrots and spices, are typical of the cuisine of Andalucía. *Ternera a la Sevillana*, veal in a sherry sauce with green olives, is a speciality of Sevilla. Rabbit *(conejo)* or hare *(liebre)* in white wine forms the basis of many a tasty casserole. Steak and various cuts of beef are also available. A local variation on this international standard is *bistec a la mantequilla de anchoas* (beefsteak with an anchovy butter sauce).

Cheese and Dessert

Spaniards eat cheese *(queso)* – notably the tangy *queso de manchego* and the milder *queso de Burgos* – after the main course. You may also come across *queso de cabrales*, a combination cheese made from goat's, cow's and sheep's milk in the northwestern province of Asturias. After ageing, it becomes blue-veined and has a sharp taste similar to Roquefort. *Idiázabal* is a smoked and cured goat's cheese.

Fruits in season include *uvas* (grapes), *higos* (figs), *melón* (melon), *naranjas* (oranges), *melocotón* (peaches), *chirimoyas* (custard apples), *fresas* (strawberries) and *cerezas* (cherries). Besides ice cream, southern Spain offers pastries and cream desserts in abundance. One appealing preparation is *brazo de gitano* (gypsy's arm), a rolled sponge cake with rum-flavoured cream filling. The ubiquitous *flan*, or egg and caramel custard, appears on menus all over Spain. Eggs cooked with sugar make a thickened custard called *natillas*.

Wine and Spirits

The white wines of Rioja are very drinkable, but the Rioja reds are the glory of Spain; the aged Gran Reservas (at least five years old) are comparable to some of France's noblest red wines, though Riojas have a character all of their own. Labels to look out for include Marqués de Riscal, Siglo, Cune, Berberana and Campo Viejo.

Navarra, north of the Ebro Valley, produces some interesting red wines (look for Campanas, Señorio de Sarría and Murchante). From La Mancha, between Madrid and Andalucía, come light, crisp Valdepeñas wines.

Fresh fruit is widely available throughout the summer

Reds and whites from Catalonia will also appear on wine lists. Labels to look for include Torres and Rene Barbier. Many restaurants have their own inexpensive table wine *(vino de la casa)* that can prove to be a less expensive, but still acceptable alternative. Catalonia also produces a sparkling wine, called *cava*. Some varieties may be rather sweet for northern palates but the Cordorniu or Freixenet *brut* (very dry) *cava* are both excellent.

Sangría, the iced combination of red wine and brandy with lemon, orange and apple slices, makes a great refresher, although its sweet and innocent taste can mask its strength.

An aristocrat among wines, *Jerez* (sherry) is produced from grapes grown in the chalky vineyards around Jerez de la Frontera. It is aged in casks by blending the young wine with a transfusion of mature sherry, a method known as *solera*. *Fino*, the driest of sherries, is a light, golden aperitif that should be served chilled. A type of *fino* called *manzanilla* is slightly richer; Sanlúcar de Barrameda *manzanilla* is especially good. *Amontillado*, usually medium dry, is a deeper gold in colour, and is heavier than a true *fino*. *Amoroso* is medium sweet, with an amber colour, and *oloroso* is still more full-bodied. Cream sherries are not popular in Spain.

The Andalucían region produces several other semi-sweet to sweet wines, most notably the sweet, mahogany-coloured wine of Málaga, called *Málaga Dulce* (rather like port), and the wines of Montilla-Moriles, near Córdoba.

Spanish brandy, or *coñac*, tends to be heavy, but it is usually drinkable and reasonably priced. The more expensive brands are much smoother.

Light refreshments alfresco in the Old Town, Granada

To Help You Order

Could we have a table?	¿nos puede dar una mesa?
Do you have a set menu?	¿tiene un menú del día?
I'd like a/an/some …	quisiera …

beer	**una cerveza**	milk	**leche**
bread	**pan**	mineral water	**agua mineral**
coffee	**un café**	napkin	**una servilleta**
cutlery	**los cubiertos**	potatoes	**patatas**
dessert	**un postre**	rice	**arroz**
fish	**pescado**	salad	**una ensalada**
fruit	**fruta**	sandwich	**un bocadillo**
glass	**un vaso**	sugar	**azúcar**
ice cream	**un helado**	tea	**un té**
meat	**carne**	(iced) water	**agua (fresca)**
menu	**la carta**	wine	**vino**

… and Read the Menu

aceitunas	olives	**judías**	beans
albóndigas	meatballs	**lenguado**	sole
almejas	baby clams	**mariscos**	shellfish
atún	tuna	**mejillones**	mussels
bacalao	cod	**ostras**	oysters
besugo	sea bream	**pastel**	cake
bistec	steak	**pimiento**	sweet red pepper
calamares	squid		
callos	tripe	**pollo**	chicken
cangrejo	crab	**pulpitos**	baby octopus
cerdo	pork	**salchichón**	salami
champiñones	mushrooms	**salmonete**	red mullet
chuletas	chops	**salsa**	sauce
cordero	lamb	**ternera**	veal
entremeses	hors-d'œuvres	**tortilla**	omelette
gambas	prawns	**trucha**	trout
huevos	eggs	**uvas**	grapes

HANDY TRAVEL TIPS

An A–Z Summary of Practical Information

A

ACCOMMODATION (*hotel; alojamiento; see also* CAMPING, YOUTH HOSTELS and RECOMMENDED HOTELS)

If you are travelling independently, you will find a wide range of accommodation in the Costa del Sol. For a comprehensive listing of accommodation and rates throughout Spain, consult the *Guía Oficial de Hoteles*, available from the Spanish National Tourist Office and some local bookshops. By law, room rates must be posted in every hotel's reception area and rooms. Meals (including breakfast) are not usually included in this rate, and VAT (IVA in Spanish) will be added to your bill.

Establishments are graded by each of Spain's 17 autonomous governments according to the following system, with one of the following classifications plus a starred rating, depending on the depth and quality of services offered:

Hotel (H): Rated between one and five stars. The most expensive option, topped only by Hotel 5-star Gran Lujo (GL), signifying top-of-the-range accommodation.

Hotel Residencia (HR): Same as a hotel, but without a restaurant.

Motel (M): Very similar to a hotel, but in reality these establishments are few and far between.

Hotel Apartamentos (HA): Apartments within hotels and rated the same as a hotel.

Residencia Apartamentos (RA): Residential apartments without a restaurant, rated the same as a hotel.

Hostal (HS): A more modest hotel, often family-owned and operated, and rated between one and three stars. Rates overlap with the lower range of hotels, eg, a three-star *hostal* usually costs about the same as a one- or two-star hotel.

Hostal Residencia (HSR): Similar to a *hostal*, but with no restaurant.

Pensión (P): A boarding house, rated between one and three stars, with only basic amenities.

Fonda (F): A small inn, fairly inexpensive, usually clean and unpretentious.

Casa de Huéspedes (CH): A guesthouse. Bottom of the scale, but usually clean and comfortable as well as cheap.

Ciudad de Vacaciones (CV): A hotel complex complete with sports facilities.

Casa Rural: Country house offering bed-and-breakfast or self-catering accommodation.

Parador: A state-run hotel, often in a castle or other historic building, generally located outside towns and in rural areas. Advance booking is not essential, but is highly recommended. For information and bookings in the UK, contact Keytel International, 402 Edgware Road, London W2 1ED; tel: 020 7616 0300; fax: 020 7616 0317. In the USA and Canada, contact Marketing Ahead, 433 Fifth Avenue, New York, NY 10016; tel: 800-223-1356 or (212) 686-9213; fax: (212) 686-0271; <mahrep@aol.com>. In Spain, contact the Paradores de Turismo, Central de Reservas, Requena 3, 28013 Madrid; tel: 915 590 069; fax: 915 593 233.

I'd like a single/double room with bath/shower	**Quisiera una habitación sencilla/doble con baño/ducha**
What's the rate per night?	**¿Cuál es el precio por noche?**

AIRPORTS (*aeropuerto; see also* GETTING THERE)

The Costa del Sol is served by Málaga's **Aeropuerto Internacional** (tel: 952 240 000), situated some 8km (5 miles) west of the centre of Málaga and 7km (4½ miles) from Torremolinos. There is a bus service every 20 minutes to Málaga, Torremolinos and Benalmádena Costa, as well as a half-hourly train service (follow the signs marked *ferrocarril*) to central Málaga and the coastal resorts from Torremolinos to Fuengirola. Taxis can be found at the taxi rank outside the terminal. The journey from the airport to central Málaga or Torremolinos takes about 10 to 15 minutes, and about 20 minutes to Fuengirola.

Other airports with international flights serving the region are at Gibraltar (tel: 350 73026) and Sevilla's San Pablo (tel: 954 449 000). Buses operate between the latter and the Puerta de Jerez, directly in front of the impressive Hotel Alfonso XIII.

B

BICYCLE AND MOPED HIRE *(bicicletas/velomotores de alquiler)*

Bicycles can be hired in most places on a daily or weekly basis. Rates for mopeds are considerably higher. Insurance is obligatory and costs extra, and a deposit will also be required. A special motorbike permit is needed for machines of over 50cc, and the wearing of crash helmets is compulsory.

I'd like to hire a bicycle What's the charge per day/week?	**Quisiera alquilar una bicicleta** **¿Cuánto cobran por día/** ** semana?**

BUDGETING FOR YOUR TRIP

To enable you to estimate the cost of your holiday, here's a list of some average prices in euros. They can only be approximate, however, as prices vary from place to place, and inflation in Spain creeps up relentlessly. Prices quoted may be subject to IVA, at variable rates.

Accommodation: Rates for a double room can range from as low as €25–30 at a *pensión* or *hostal* to as much as €400 at a top-of-the-range, luxury 5-star hotel. As a rule of thumb, a nice 4-star hotel will cost between €90 and €120. Some hotels may have three or four pricing seasons. For example, in Sevilla during the Easter

Week celebrations and the subsequent *Feria de Abril*, rates can be double what you would normally be charged.

Car hire: Prices vary dramatically depending on whether you hire before your trip starts; whether you hire from a company in your own country or locally; how long you hire for; whether you want an automatic or manual transmission vehicle; and what insurance coverage you want, or are obliged, to purchase.

If you want a small, manual transmission car primarily for local use, then it may be cheaper to rent from a local company on the Costa del Sol. However, for North American visitors who plan on driving extensively or require a car with automatic transmission, **Auto Europe** (tel: 888-223-5555) will invariably offer the best rates.

Entertainment: A cinema ticket costs around €5, a flamenco nightclub (entry and first drink) starts at around €20, and a disco from €6. Amusement parks cost around €25 per adult or €18 per child per day. A bullfight ticket ranges from €20 to €100.

Meals and drinks: These vary considerably, depending on where you are. In a bar, a Continental breakfast will cost around €4. The cheapest three-course meal with one drink, a *menú del día* in a small bar or restaurant, will be around €7. Dinner in a moderately-priced restaurant will be about €20 per person, including wine. At the top restaurants, expect to pay up to €50 or more per person, plus wine.

In a bar, a draught beer (a *caña*) or a small bottle will range from €0.60 to €1, a coffee around €1, a Spanish brandy from €1.50 to €2, a soft drink from €1 and a glass of local wine about €1. Sitting at an outside table usually means you pay more for a drink than if you sit inside at the bar.

Shopping: Again, prices can vary substantially. By far the cheapest places are the large hypermarkets such as Pryca where, for example, a can of San Miguel beer might cost around €0.50. In a small corner store or *supermercado* (supermarket) the same beer might cost about €0.75 and similar price differentials exist for most other goods.

Sightseeing: Tickets to the major sights, such as Sevilla's Real Alcáza and Córdoba's Mezquita cost around €5; and the Alhambra in Granada €7. Admission prices for most museums, galleries, cathedrals etc. are far more modest.

Sports: Per-day green fees for golf range from around €45 up to as much as €180 at the very top courses. Tennis court fees start at €6 per hour. Horse riding starts at about €12 per hour.

Taxis: Taxis are generally inexpensive, with a typical city-centre trip costing around €3. It's best to establish the rate for a long-distance journey before you depart. There are fixed rates, well displayed, for all destinations from Málaga's international airport.

Train: The *cercanía* (local) line between Málaga and Fuengirola is a fast, clean and inexpensive way to travel along this part of the Costa del Sol. A return (round-trip) ticket costs €4. A single ticket aboard the TRD train from Málaga to Sevilla costs €13.60.

C

CAMPING

There are numerous official campsites along the Costa del Sol and throughout Andalucía. Facilities vary, but most have electricity and running water, and many have shops and children's playgrounds. Some even have laundrettes and restaurants. Rates depend on the facilities available. For a complete list of campsites, consult the *Guía de Campings*, available from the Spanish National Tourist Office and some local bookshops.

Camping outside of official sites is permitted, provided you obtain permission from the landowner. However, you are not allowed to pitch your tent on tourist beaches, in urban areas, or within 1km (½ mile) of an official site.

May we camp here?	**¿Podemos acampar aquí?**

CAR HIRE (RENTAL) (*coches de alquiler; see also* DRIVING)

Unless you plan to stay in one of the remote parts of the Costa del Sol, or are touring extensively, a car is superfluous to your requirements. In fact, if you are based at one of the popular resorts or major cities, having a car is more of a disadvantage than an advantage (it's hard to find places to park and there's always the possibility that your car will be broken into). But if you do want to hire a car there are numerous deals available via the Internet, and they can often be booked at the same time as your flight. For North American visitors, **Auto Europe** (tel: 888-223-5555) is the largest organisation and usually offers the best rates available, especially if you want a car with automatic transmission. Otherwise, there are numerous firms operating in the cities and resorts on the Costa del Sol, including the major international companies at the airports and some railway stations; rates vary enormously.

Comprehensive insurance coverage should be considered a necessity, even if it doesn't come as part of the package. Theft from cars is rampant in this region, and extra coverage against the theft of the radio and other car parts and damage caused by thieves is very reasonable and seriously worth considering.

Normally, you must be over 21 to hire a car and you will need a valid driving licence that you have held for at least 12 months, your passport and a major credit card – cash deposits are high and are not always accepted. Visitors from countries other than the US, Canada and those in the EU may be expected to present an International Driver's Licence.

I'd like to hire a car (tomorrow) for one day/a week	**Quisiera alquilar un coche (para mañana) por un día/una semana**
Please include full insurance coverage	**Haga el favor de incluir el seguro a todo riesgo**

CLIMATE

Plenty of hot sunshine and cloudless skies are the rule, not the exception, on the Costa del Sol, and in most parts of Andalucía, too. But there are seasonal variations worth noting when you choose your holiday. From June to September, hot days with low humidity are followed by slightly cooler evenings; rain is a rarity. In April, May and October, daytime temperatures remain quite warm, but it can get cold at night. From November to March, sunshine can still be enjoyed, but may be interrupted by chill winds from the mountains and even rain – on average four to six rainy days a month in winter – so be prepared.

Inland, the climate is different. The triangle between Sevilla, Córdoba and Granada is the hottest in Europe, with summertime temperatures often well over 38°C (100°F). And the presence of the towering Sierra Nevada Mountains near Granada ensures that the city and surrounding area see snow in the winter.

The average monthly temperatures for Málaga are:

	J	F	M	A	M	J	J	A	S	O	N	D
max.°C	16	17	18	20	23	25	28	29	26	23	19	17
min.°C	10	11	12	13	15	18	20	21	19	17	14	11
max.°F	60	62	65	68	73	78	83	83	79	73	66	62
min.°F	50	51	54	56	60	64	68	69	67	62	57	53
sea °C	15	14	15	16	17	21	21	23	21	18	17	14
°F	59	57	59	60	62	69	69	73	69	65	62	57

CLOTHING

From June to September the days are always hot and lightweight cotton clothes are the order of the day. During the rest of the year, a light jacket and a raincoat or umbrella will come in handy. Warmer attire will be needed in Granada and the Sierra Nevada during the winter. Respectable (i.e. modest) clothing should, of course, be worn when visiting churches, although women are no longer expected to cover their heads.

COMPLAINTS

By law, all hotels and restaurants must have official complaint forms *(hoja de reclamaciones)* and produce them on demand. The original of this triplicate document should be sent to the Ministry of Tourism; one copy remains with the establishment involved and one copy is given to you. The very act of asking for the *hoja* may resolve the problem in itself, as the establishment knows that tourism authorities take a serious view of such complaints.

CRIME AND SAFETY

Spain's crime rate has increased in recent years, especially in the cities and some of the larger resorts. Here are a few precautions. Always carry a minimum of cash and keep your passport, travellers' cheques, credit cards and cash in a money belt or, better still, in your hotel safe. Never leave bags unattended, or even out of reach. Lock your car and stow any possessions out of sight in the boot and never leave anything in your car overnight. All thefts must be reported to the police within 24 hours and you will need a copy of the police report in order to make a claim on your insurance.

As a precaution, photocopy the relevant pages of your passport and airline ticket and keep them in a separate place from the originals. If your passport is stolen, your consulate should be informed *(see* EMBASSIES AND CONSULATES*)*.

CUSTOMS *(aduana)* AND ENTRY REQUIREMENTS

Most visitors, including citizens of EU countries, the US, Canada, Ireland, Australia and New Zealand require only a valid passport – no visa, no health certificate – to enter Spain. Visitors from South Africa, however, must have a visa. Further information as well as the visa itself can be obtained from the Spanish Consulate General,

37 Short Market Street, Cape Town, 8001; tel: (27) 21 422-2415; fax: (27) 21 422-2328. They are open Mon–Fri 8am–1.30pm.

Currency restrictions: Tourists are allowed to bring an unlimited amount of euros or foreign currency into the country. On departure you must declare any amount beyond the equivalent of 6,000 euros.

D

DRIVING

Drive on the right, overtake on the left. Give way to traffic coming from the right.

Road conditions: Main roads and motorways are generally very good and improving all the time; secondary roads less so. New bypasses around Málaga and the coastal resorts have vastly improved conditions on the N340/E15. There is a new stretch of motorway, the A7, between Málaga and Estepona. The road between Motril and Almería is still narrow and twisting and plagued with slow-moving lorries.

Rules and regulations: Speed limits are 50kph (30mph) in built-up areas, 90–100kph (55–60mph) on highways and 120kph (75mph) on motorways. Note that Spanish drivers tend to sound their horn or flash their headlights when overtaking. The use of seat belts (front and back seats) is obligatory. A red warning triangle must be carried. Motorcycle riders and their passengers must wear crash helmets. Spanish roads are patrolled by the motorcycle police of the *Guardia Civil*. They can impose on-the-spot fines for common offences including speeding, overtaking without flashing your lights, travelling too close to the car in front and driving with burned-out lights.

Fuel: Service stations are plentiful, but it's a good idea to keep an eye on the gauge in more remote areas, like the Alpujarra.

Parking *(aparcamiento)*: Parking regulations are strictly enforced – offending vehicles will be towed away and a hefty fine

charged for their return. A yellow-painted curb means parking is pro-
hibited at all times; blue means parking is restricted to certain times.

If you need help: The Civil Guard is efficient with minor mechani-
cal problems and go out of their way to help you if you have a
breakdown. Spanish garages are also efficient, but in tourist areas
major repairs may take several days because of heavy workload.
Spare parts are readily available for most major makes of cars.

Road signs: Most of the road signs used in Spain are international
pictograms. But here are some written signs you will come across:

Autopista (de peaje)	(Toll) motorway (expressway)
Ceda el paso	Give way
Circunvalación	Bypass/ring-road
Curva peligrosa	Dangerous bend
Despacio	Slow
Desviación	Diversion
Obras	Road works
Peligro	Danger
Prohibido aparcar	No parking
Salida de camiones	Truck exit
Sin plomo	Unleaded petrol
Can I park here?	**¿Se puede aparcar aquí?**
Full tank, please, top grade	**Llénelo, por favor, con super**
Please check the oil/tyres/ battery	**Por favor, controle el aceite/ los neumáticos/la batería**
There's been an accident	**Ha habido un accidente**

E

ELECTRICITY *(corriente eléctrica)*

220v/50Hz AC is now standard, but older installations of 125
volts can still occur in places. An adapter for Continental-style

two-pin sockets will be needed, and American 110v appliances will also require a transformer.

EMBASSIES AND CONSULATES *(embajadas y consulados)*

Australia: Federico Rubio 14, 41004 Sevilla; tel: 954 220 971.
Canada: Edificio Horizonte, Calle Cervantes, Málaga; tel: 952 223 346; Avenida de los Pinos 34, Casa 4 Mairena del Aljarafe, Sevilla; tel: 954 768 828.
Republic of Ireland: Avenida de los Boliches 15, Fuengirola; tel: 952 475 108. Plaza de Santa Cruz, 6-Baja, Sevilla; tel: 954 216 361.
UK: Edificio Duquesa, Calle Duquesa de Parcent 8, Málaga; tel: 952 217 571; Plaza Nueva 8-B, Sevilla; tel: 954 228 874.
US: Centro Comercial Las Rampas II, Fuengirola; tel: 952 474 891. Paseo de Las Delicias 7, Sevilla; tel: 954 231 885.

EMERGENCIES *(emergencias)*

Unless you are fluent in Spanish, you should seek help through your hotel receptionist or the local tourist office. If you can speak Spanish, the following telephone numbers may be useful:

	Ambulance	Police	Sea Rescue
Spain	061	091	900202202
Gibraltar	199	199	

G

GETTING THERE *(see also* AIRPORTS*)*

By Air
From the UK: Numerous scheduled and charter flights link the main UK airports with Málaga. There are also flights to Sevilla, although not so many. Check the travel sections of the Sunday papers or book online for some good deals. Many people travel to the Costa del Sol on an all-inclusive package holiday, which is usually the most inexpensive way of doing it.

From North America: At the time of writing, only one US-based airline has a direct, scheduled flight to the Costa del Sol and Andalucía, although some charter flights fly directly, with a change of planes in Madrid.

Iberia (tel: 800-772-4642; <www.iberia.com>) has flights from New York City and Miami to Madrid and connections from there to Málaga, Sevilla and other smaller airports. Air Europa (tel: 718-244-7055; fax: 718-656-0408; <www.air-europa.com>) has flights from New York City to Madrid and connections from there to Málaga, Sevilla and other smaller airports. It also has a round-trip weekly flight between New York City and Málaga. In addition, Spanair (tel: 888-545-5757; <www.spanair.com/en>) flies out of Washington, DC and has flights to Madrid with onward connections to Málaga and Sevilla. Spanair also offers the economical Spain Pass, good for travel on the mainland and to the Canary Islands.

By Car

From the UK, the main route from the French ferry ports runs south through western France to Bordeaux and into Spain at Irún, west of the Pyrenees. Continue on the A8 via San Sebastián and then the A1/NI/E5 all the way to Madrid, via Burgos. Continue through Madrid on the M30 and then take the A4/NIV/E5 south to Bailén. From there, either continue on the NIV/E5 westwards to Córdoba and Sevilla and then on the A4/E5 to Cádiz via Jerez de la Frontera; or take the N323/E902 south via Jaén to Granada then go directly south to the coast at Motril, or follow the A329/A359/N331 south to Málaga.

Alternatively, take the eastern route through France to Perpignan in the southeast and follow the A7 motorway south via Barcelona, Tarragona, Valencia and Alicante to Murcia. From Murcia continue to Puerto Lumbreras and take the E15/N340 to Almería, Málaga and around the Atlantic coast to Cádiz. From Cádiz, you can take the A4/E5 via Jerez de la Frontera to Sevilla.

Your driving time (three steady days by either route) can be cut by using the long-distance car-ferry service from Plymouth to Santander or Portsmouth to Bilbao in northern Spain *(see below)*. From Santander or Bilbao, follow the road to Burgos and proceed as above.

By Rail

From the UK, take the high-speed Eurostar service (<www.eurostar.com>) from London's Waterloo International Station through the Channel Tunnel to Paris Gare du Nord. French National Railways, SNCF (<www.sncf.com>), operates high-speed TGV trains from either Gare Montparnasse or Gare d'Orleans to the French/Spanish border at Hendaye/Irún or Cerbere/Port Bou on the west and east sides of the Pyrenees respectively. From Irún, change to a Spanish Madrid-bound RENFE train or the direct, but very slow, *Tren Media Luna* to Algeciras. From Port Bou, you'll take a fast TALGO train, continuing on to Madrid either via Zaragoza or Valencia.

Alternatively, take a RENFE hotel train *(hotel tren)* from Paris to Madrid (Francisco de Goya) or Barcelona (Joan Miró). From Madrid (Puerta de Atocha), take either the high-speed AVE train to Córdoba and on to Sevilla, or the fast express T200 service to Córdoba and on to Málaga.

Other international *hotel tren* services are between Lisbon and Madrid (Lusitania); Milan and Barcelona (Salvador Dalí); and Zurich and Barcelona (Pau Casals).

By Sea

From the UK, two companies offer car-ferry services to mainland Spain, with schedules varying by the season. Brittany Ferries (tel: 0870 901 2400; <www.brittany-ferries.com>) has sailings between Plymouth and Santander (average crossing time 24 hours). P&O European Ferries (tel: 0870 242 4999; <www.poportsmouth.com>) has sailings between Portsmouth and Bilbao (average crossing time 35 hours). Motorists can then drive from Santander or Bilbao to

Burgos and then continue south, using the directions in the BY CAR section *on page 116*, to the Costa del Sol and Andalucía.

GUIDES AND TOURS

English-speaking guides can be hired through local tourist offices (*see* TOURIST INFORMATION *on page 127*). Guided tours and excursions can be booked at most hotels or through any of the numerous travel agencies *(agencia de viaje).*

H

HEALTH AND MEDICAL CARE

Anything other than basic emergency treatment can be very expensive and you should not leave home without adequate insurance, preferably including coverage for an emergency flight home in the event of serious injury or illness.

Citizens of EU countries are entitled to free emergency hospital treatment. In order to qualify, you should obtain form E111 from a post office before you leave. You may have to pay all or part of the price of treatment or any medicine you require; keep receipts so that you can claim a refund when you return home.

The main health hazard on the Costa del Sol is also its biggest attraction – the sun. Take a sun hat, sunglasses and plenty of high-factor sunscreen, and limit your sunbathing sessions to an hour or less until you begin to tan.

For minor ailments, visit the local first-aid post *(ambulatorio)*. Away from your hotel, don't hesitate to ask the police or a tourist information office for help. At your hotel, ask the staff for assistance. *Farmacias* (chemists) are usually open during normal shopping hours. After hours, at least one *farmacia* in every town remains open all night. Called a *farmacia de guardia,* its location is posted in the window of all other *farmacias* and in the local newspapers.

Where's the nearest (all-night) chemist?	**¿Dónde está la farmacia (de guardia) más cercana?**
I need a doctor/dentist	**Necesito un médico/dentista**
I feel unwell	**Me siento mal**
It hurts here	**Me duele aquí**
I have a temperature	**Tengo fiebre**
sunburn/sunstroke	**quemadura del sol/ una insolación**
an upset stomach	**molestias de estómago**

HOLIDAYS *(días festivos)*

Andalucía celebrates its regional holiday on 28 February, and banks, post offices, government offices and many other businesses are also closed on the following dates. Note that there are a number of local and regional holidays and saints' days too; check with the local tourist office.

1	**January**	*Año Nuevo*	New Year's Day
6	**January**	*Epifanía*	Epiphany
19	**March**	*San José*	St Joseph's Day
1	**May**	*Día del Trabajo*	Labour Day
25	**July**	*Santiago Apóstol*	St James's Day
15	**August**	*Asunción*	Assumption Day
12	**October**	*Día de la Hispanidad*	Columbus Day
1	**November**	*Todos los Santos*	All Saints' Day
6	**December**	*Día de la Constitución*	Constitution Day
8	**December**	*Inmaculada Concepción*	Immaculate Conception
25	**December**	*Día de Navidad*	Christmas Day

Movable dates:

Jueves Santo	Maundy Thursday; late March–mid-April
Viernes Santo	Good Friday; late March–mid-April
Corpus Christi	mid-June

L

LANGUAGE

The national language of Spain, Castilian, is spoken in the Costa del Sol and Andalucía. Throughout Andalucía, the local dialect Andaluz, which is a little more difficult to understand, is commonly used. English is widely spoken in the resort towns, though it is helpful to learn at least a few basic phrases in Castilian. The *Berlitz Spanish Phrasebook and Dictionary* covers most situations you are likely to encounter, and the *Berlitz Spanish-English/English-Spanish Pocket Dictionary* contains some 12,500 entries, plus a menu-reader supplement.

M

MEDIA (*see also* WEBSITES)

Radio and television (*radio; televisión*): There are several local radio stations that broadcast in English on the FM band, such as Central FM (98.6 and 103.8), Onda Cero Marbella (101.6), Coastline Radio (97.7), Spectrum (105.5) and Premiere Network Radio (96.8 and 107.0). Radio broadcasts can also be picked up from Gibraltar. Network television programmes are all in Spanish, but better hotels and many English bars also have satellite TV with CNN, MTV, Superchannel, Sky TV etc.

Newspapers and magazines (*periódicos, revistas*): In the major tourist areas you can buy most European newspapers on the day of publication, with some English ones even having Spanish editions, but at about three times the price. The *International Herald Tribune* is also widely available as are all kinds of British and American magazines. The weekly *Sur in English,* available free, is aimed at residents on the Costa del Sol and carries local news and events. The *Costa Del Sol News* is another English-language newspaper that is published every Thursday. It offers entertainment listings as well as information about religious services in the area, and has a particularly useful page called *Costa Fun...What's On and Where to Go* that provides comprehensive information about all the tourist attractions along the Costa del Sol and Gibraltar.

MONEY

Currency: The euro (EUR) is the official currency used in Spain. Notes are denominated in 5, 10, 20, 50, 100 and 500 euros; coins in 1 and 2 euros and 1, 2, 5, 10, 20 and 50 cents.

Currency Exchange: Outside of normal banking hours, many travel agencies and other businesses displaying a *cambio* sign will change foreign currency into euros. Larger hotels will also change guests' money. The exchange rate is slightly worse than at the bank. Travellers' cheques always get a better rate than cash. Take your passport when changing money or travellers' cheques, for identification purposes.

I want to change some pounds/dollars	**Quiero cambiar libras/dólares**
Do you accept travellers' cheques?	**¿Acepta usted cheque de viajero?**
Can I pay with this credit card?	**¿Puedo pagar con esta tarjeta de crédito?**

ATMs: ATMs *(telebancos)* can be found almost everywhere, and from them you can draw funds in euros against your bank account with a credit or debit card.

Credit cards: All the internationally recognised cards are accepted by hotels, restaurants and businesses in Spain.

VAT *(IVA)*: Remember that IVA *(impuesto sobre el valor agregado)*, the Spanish equivalent of value added tax, will be added to your hotel and restaurant bills; it currently stands at 7 percent. A higher rate of 16 percent applies to car-hire charges and a rate of 4 percent applies to certain basic necessities.

O

OPENING HOURS

Shops and offices and other businesses generally observe the afternoon siesta, opening 9am–1.30 or 2pm, and 4.30 or 5pm–7.30 or 8pm, but in tourist areas many places now stay open all day. Banks are generally open 9am–2pm, but will, of course, be closed on the numerous public holidays.

P

POLICE *(policía)*

There are three separate police forces in Spain. The *Policía Municipal*, who are attached to the local town hall and usually wear blue uniforms, are the ones to whom you should report theft and other crimes. The *Policía Nacional* is a national anti-crime unit wearing dark-blue uniforms; and the *Guardia Civil*, with green uniforms, is a national force whose most conspicuous role is as a highway patrol. Spanish police officers, often working in pairs, are generally very courteous and helpful towards foreign visitors.

The emergency number is **911**.

POST OFFICES *(correos)*

Post offices handle mail and telegrams only; normally, you cannot make telephone calls from them. Routine postal business is generally transacted 8.30am–2.30pm Mon–Fri, and 9.30am–1pm Sat. Postage stamps *(sellos)* can also be bought at tobacconists *(estancos)*, at hotel desks and at tourist shops selling postcards. Mail for destinations outside Spain should be posted in the box marked *extranjero* (overseas), and delivery is slow.

PUBLIC TRANSPORT

By Bus *(autobús)*: Buses are an excellent form of transport, not just along the Costa del Sol but throughout Andalucía. They reach many destinations that the train doesn't, and when they do serve the same places, they are often cheaper, faster and more frequent. Automóviles Portillo (tel: 952 247 314) operates a service every half-hour from Málaga that connects Torremolinos (tel: 952 382 419), Benalmádena-Costa (tel: 952 443 563), Fuengirola (tel: 952 475 066), Marbella (tel: 952 772 192), San Pedro Alcántara (tel: 952 781 396) and Estepona (tel: 952 800 249). Alsina Graells Sur (tel: 952 318 295) operates daily service between Málaga and Sevilla (tel: 954 417 111), Granada (tel: 958 251 350), Córdoba (tel: 957 236 474), Almería (tel: 950 221 888) and La Linea de la Concepción (tel: 956 102 396), a short walk from the border with Gibraltar.

Where is the (nearest) bus stop?	**¿Dónde está la parada de autobuses (más cercana)?**
When's the next bus/ boat for…?	**¿A qué hora sale el próximo autobús/barco para…?**
I want a ticket to…	**Quiero un billete para…**
single (one-way)	**ida**
return (round-trip)	**ida y vuelta**
Will you tell me when to get off?	**¿Podría indicarme cuándo tengo que bajar?**

By Ferry *(barco)*: Algeciras is a major port and Trasmediterránea (tel: 956 665 200; <www.trasmediterranea.com>) is the largest company operating from there. It has frequent sailings, on high-speed or regular ferries, to Ceuta (tel: 956 509 552), a Spanish enclave on the Moroccan coast, or Tangier, Morocco (tel: 09-941 101). It also operates a daily ferry on the much longer routes from Málaga (tel: 952 243 910; no service Friday) and Almería (tel: 952

236 155) to Melilla (tel: 952 681 244), the other Spanish enclave on the Moroccan coast. There is also a very limited ferry service between Gibraltar and Tangier.

By Taxi *(taxi)*: Taxis in the major cities have meters, but in villages along the rest of the coast they usually don't, so it's a good idea to check the fare before you get in. If you take a long trip, you will be charged a two-way fare whether you make the return journey or not. By law a taxi may carry only four people. A green light and/or a *libre* (free) sign indicates that a taxi is available. You can telephone for a cab as well. The numbers to call are as follows: in Benalmádena, tel: 244 15 45; in Estepona, tel: 280 29 00; in Fuengirola, tel: 247 10 00; in Málaga, tel: 232 79 50; in Marbella, tel: 277 05 03; in Torremolinos, tel: 238 06 00; and in Gibraltar, tel: 70027.

By Train *(tren)*: A suburban *(cercanías)* rail service runs along the coast between downtown Málaga (the Centro-Alameda station) and Fuengirola; tel: 952 478 540. It includes stops at the RENFE train station, the international airport in Málaga, Torremolinos (tel: 952 360 202) and Benalmádena (tel: 952 360 202). Trains depart from Málaga every 30 minutes between 6am and 10.30pm. From Fuengirola, there is half-hourly service between 6.45am and 11.05pm.

From the mainline (RENFE) station in Málaga (tel: 952 360 202), there is service to Ronda (tel: 952 871 673) and on to Algeciras. From Córdoba (tel: 957 400 202), Granada (tel: 958 271 272) and Sevilla Santa Justa (tel: 954 540 202), there are connections to other destinations in Andalucía. There are also long-distance *(largo recorrido)* trains via Córdoba to Madrid and Barcelona. Timetables and information are available from railway stations and tourist offices, and from the RENFE website <www.renfe.es>.

Train Passes: For information on the Spain Flexipass, Spain Rail 'n' Drive Pass, point-to-point rail tickets on Spanish trains, including the high-speed Euromed (Barcelona, Valencia, Alicante) or AVE (Madrid, Córdoba, Sevilla, Cádiz, Málaga) trains, American visitors should contact Rail Europe (tel: 888-382-7245; <www.raileurope.com>), *before* leaving for Europe.

The Spain Flexipass gives you three days of unlimited rail travel in 1st or 2nd class, starting at US$155. Additional days are US$30 (2nd class) and US$35 (1st class) each. The Spain Rail 'n' Drive Pass gives you three days of unlimited rail travel plus two days of car rental. Prices depend on class of rail travel and car category (four categories are available) and start at US$255 per person for two travelling together.

R

RELIGION

Spain is a Roman Catholic country. Mass is conducted in English in Benalmádena Costa at the Virgen del Carmen (Sol y Mar) at 10am every Sunday and feast day, and at Los Boliches in the St Andrew's Chapel, Edificio Jupiter, Avenida Jesús Santos Rein, every Saturday at 5.45pm. Many Protestant denominations such as the Church of England (Episcopal), Church of Scotland (Presbyterian) and the Methodist church are represented on the Costa del Sol. In addition, there are congregations of Christian Scientists, Jehovah's Witnesses and Mormons here. Muslim mosques can be found in Málaga, Fuengirola and Marbella, and there are a number of synagogues in Marbella and Torremolinos. For services, refer to *Sur in English*, page 2, or contact the local tourist office.

T

TELEPHONE *(teléfono)*

The country code for Spain is 34. To reach an international operator from Spain, dial 025. The country code for the US. and Canada is 1;

for the UK 44; for Australia 61; for New Zealand 64; for the Republic of Ireland 353; and for South Africa 27.

In addition to the telephone office, *Telefónica*, in Málaga and other major towns and cities, there are phone booths everywhere from which you can make local and international calls. Instructions in English and area codes for different countries are displayed in the booths. International calls are expensive, so be sure to have a plentiful supply of suitable euro coins. Some telephones accept credit cards, and many require a phone card *(tarjeta telefónica)*, available from a tobacconist and some shops where you will see a sign outside. To call overseas, pick up the receiver, wait for the dial tone, then dial 00. Wait for a second tone, then dial the country code, area code (minus the initial zero) and number.

Remember, calling directly from your hotel room is almost always prohibitively expensive unless you are using a calling card. If you're from the US or Canada, your long-distance carrier should have a free connection number you can dial for access. Be sure to determine what it is before you depart your home country, since the number is different for each country and is often difficult to obtain once you are in the Costa del Sol.

Can you get me this number? **¿Puede comunicarme con este número?**

TIME DIFFERENCES

Spanish time coincides with most of Western Europe – Greenwich Mean Time plus one hour. In summer, another hour is added for daylight saving time.

New York	London	**Spain**	Sydney	Auckland
6am	11am	**noon**	8pm	10pm

TIPPING

Since a service charge is normally included in hotel and restaurant bills, tipping is not obligatory, but 10 percent can be added if service was exceptional. About 10 percent of the bill is usual for taxi drivers and hairdressers and others offering personal services. In a bar it is usual to leave some small change to round up the bill.

TOILETS

There are many expressions for toilets in Spanish: *aseos, servicios, baños, sanitarios, WC* and *retretes*; the first two are the most common. Just about every bar and restaurant has a toilet available for public use, but it is polite to buy a drink in the bar. The usual signs are *Damas* for women and *Caballeros* for men, though you might also see *Señoras* and *Señores*.

TOURIST INFORMATION OFFICES *(oficinas de turismo)*

Information may be obtained from one of the international branches of the Spanish National Tourist Office, as listed below.

Canada: 2 Bloor Street West, 34th Floor, Toronto, Ontario M4W 3E2; tel: 416-961-3131; fax: 416-961-1992; email: <spainto@global serve.net>.

UK: 22–23 Manchester Square, London, W1M 5AP; tel: 020 7486 8077; fax: 020 7486 8034; brochure line: 0891 669 920; email: <londres@tourspain.es>.

US: Water Tower Place, Suite 915 East, 845 North Michigan Avenue, Chicago, IL 60611; tel: 312-642-1992; fax: 312-642-9817; email: <buzon.oficial@chicago.oet.mcx.es>.

8383 Wilshire Boulevard, Suite 960, Beverly Hills, Los Angeles, CA 90211; tel: 213-658-7188; fax: 323-658-1061; email: <buzon.oficial@losangeles.oet.mcx.es>.

665 Fifth Avenue, New York, NY 10103; tel: 212-265-8822; fax: 212-265-8864; email: <buzon.oficial@nuevayork.oet.mcx.es>.

1221 Brickell Avenue, Miami, FL 33131; tel: 305-358-1992; fax: 305-358-8223; email: <buzon.oficial@miami.oet.mcx.es>.

For more detailed information about the Costa del Sol, contact the Costa del Sol Patronato de Turismo, Palacio de Congresos Costa del Sol, Calle México s/n, 29620 Torremolinos, Málaga; tel: 952 058 694/5/6; fax: 952 050 311; email: <costadelsol@sopde.es>; <www.costadelsol.sopde.es>.

For more detailed information about Gibraltar, contact the Gibraltar Information Bureau, Duke of Kent House, Cathedral Square; tel: (350) 45000; fax: 74943.

For information about Andalucía, contact the Consejería de Turismo y Deporte Turismo Andaluz, S., Centro Internacional de Turismo Andalucía (CINTA), Ctra Nacional 340, Km189.6, 296000 Marbella, Málaga; tel: 952 838 785; fax: 952 836 369; <www.Andalucía.org>.

For more information about individual cities and towns, visit the local tourist office *(oficina de turismo)*. Offices are normally open 9am–1pm and 4–7pm, and all of them have somebody on staff who will be able to give advice and information in English. Major ones are: Granada, tel: 958 225 990; Sevilla, tel: 954 221 404; Malaga, tel: 952 213 445; Marbella, tel: 952 771 442.

V

VAT REFUNDS

The Spanish government levies a value-added tax (called *IVA*) on most items in shops (currently up to 13.8 percent). Tourists from outside the EU who spend a minimum of €100 or £60/US$100 in stores where there is a tax free shopping logo can claim a refund of the *IVA* they pay. Whenever you make a purchase, simply ask for a Global Refund Cheque, then when you declare your purchases at Customs, your cheque will be validated and can be cashed at a nearby Cash Refund Office or at any of the International Cash Refund offices worldwide. Another option that may be more convenient is to post the cheque to a Cash Refund Office and have your credit card account automatically credited. It's worthwhile if you plan on spending a lot in one place.

W

WEBSITES (*see also* ACCOMMODATION, GETTING THERE, PUBLIC TRANSPORT and TOURIST INFORMATION)

The English-language publications *Sur in English* and *Costa del Sol News* have websites that provide information about special events for visitors. Check out <www.surinenglish.com> and <costadelsolnews.es>. For general tourist information, look at <www.tourspain.com>.

WEIGHTS AND MEASURES

Like most of Europe, Spain uses the metric system.

1 metre	=	approx 39 ins
1 kilometre	=	1,093 yards or approx 0.6 mile
16 km	=	approx 10 miles
1 kilogram	=	approx 2.2 lb
1 litre	=	1.75 pints
40 litres	=	approx 9 gallons (10 US gallons)

Y

YOUTH HOSTELS (*albergues de juveniles*; *see also* ACCOMMODATION, CAMPING *and* WEBSITES)

Red de Albergues Juveniles de Andalucía provides a complete listing of all hostels on the Costa del Sol and in Andalucía on their website <www.inturjoven.com/index-uk.asp>.

Note that the Spanish word *hostal* does not mean youth hostel, but a basic hotel.

Recommended Hotels

These hotels in the Costa del Sol and Andalucía are listed alphabetically by region or town. For each one we give its Spanish hotel grade *(explained in Accommodation on page 105)* and its price category. Wheelchair accessibility is not common in Spain. Although one or two smaller hotels may cater to people with disabilities, it is generally the larger and more expensive places that have such facilities. As a basic guide we have used the symbols below to indicate prices per night for a double room with bath or shower, including service charge and taxes, during the high season. Low season rates can be considerably lower. Please note that these rates do not include breakfast. All these hotels accept major credit cards unless stated otherwise.

€€€€€	180–300 euros
€€€€	120–180 euros
€€€	90–120 euros
€€	60–90 euros
€	below 60 euros

CÁDIZ

Hotel Puertatierra (4 stars) €€ *Avenida de Andalucía 34; tel: 956 272 111; fax: 956 250 311.* Beautifully designed modern hotel with a fine location, close to both the beach and old town. All expected amenities including on-site parking. 98 rooms.

CARMONA

Hotel Casa Palacio Casa de Carmona (5 stars) €€€€ *Plaza de Lasso 1; tel: 954 143 300; fax: 954 143 752; <www.casade-carmona.com>.* A 16th-century palace carefully and lovingly renovated into a beautiful and very hospitable luxury hotel. Every room is individually decorated and filled with handpicked antiques from Madrid, London and Paris. 33 rooms.

CEUTA

Parador Hotel La Muralla (4 stars) €€€ *Plaza Ntra. Sra. de África 15; tel: 956 514 940; fax: 956 514 947.* Views to the north to Gibraltar and south over Morocco, nice gardens and pool. Built into the ancient palace walls. 106 rooms.

CÓRDOBA

Hotel NH Amistad Córdoba (4 stars) €€€ *Plaza Maimónides 3; tel: 957 420 335; fax: 957 420 365.* Located in the Jewish quarter close to the Mezquita. Two 18th-century mansions, next to the old Moorish wall, combined and restored to create a fully modernised hotel in harmony with this historic city. 84 rooms.

Hotel Macía Alfaros (4 stars) €€€ *C/ Alfaros 18; tel: 957 491 920; fax: 957 492 210, email: <alfaros@igm.es>.* In the heart of the city, this is a dignified oasis of calm in the old quarter. Moorish in style, it has elegant and fully equipped rooms, a pool, restaurants and private parking. 135 rooms.

Hotel Selu (3 stars) €€ *Eduardo Dato 7; tel: 957 476 500; fax: 957 478 376.* Modern, functional hotel located in the commercial and historic centre, close to the railway and bus stations. Facilities include a gym. 115 rooms.

ESTEPONA

Las Dunas Beach Hotel & Spa (5 star GL) €€€€€ *Ctra. Cádiz, Km163.5; tel: 952 794 345; fax: 952 794 825; <www.las-dunas.com>.* A low-rise Andalucían-style *hacienda* with Moorish influences. Soothing colour schemes inside and out; sub-tropical gardens leading to the beach; sports and health club. Luxurious rooms with terraces or sun decks offering marvellous views. 73 rooms.

Kempinski Resort Hotel (5 star) €€€€€ *Ctra de Cádiz, Km159; tel: 952 809 500; fax: 952 809 550; <www.kempinski-spain.com>.* Opened in September 1999. The rooms in this architecturally interesting hotel all have sea views. There are also subtropical gardens, a 1-km (¹/₂-mile) beach, numerous pools, water sports, horse riding, a restaurant serving haute cuisine and the Polly Vital wellness centre. 149 rooms.

Hotel La Cartuja (4 stars) €€€ *Campos de la Cartuja, Ctra Benahavis, Km1.5; tel: 952 882 270; fax: 952 882 086.* A very stylish hotel, both in terms of its architecture and furnishings, overlooking the Atalaya golf course just inland from the sea. Offers an array of suites and self-catering apartments, pools, sports facilities and a fine restaurant.

FUENGIROLA

Hotel El Puerto (3 stars) €€ *Paseo Maritimo 32; tel: 952 470 100; fax: 952 470 166.* An attractive modern circular hotel set on a prime location on the promenade at Fuengirola. It has pleasant rooms and a rooftop swimming pool with spectacular views over the Costa del Sol. 300 rooms.

GIBRALTAR

The Rock Hotel (5 stars) €€€ *Europa Road; tel: 350-73000; fax: 350-73513.* Traditional English-style hotel and restaurant with sweeping views over the bay and Strait of Gibraltar and Africa on the horizon. Nine-acre garden with a saltwater pool. 104 rooms.

GRANADA

Alhambra Palace (4 stars) €€€ *Peña Partida 2; tel: 958 221 468; fax: 958 226 404.* An impressive and elaborate Moorish-style palace in the Alhambra Park complex. Elegant rooms, delightful tearooms and terraces with stunning hilltop views over the city and up to the Sierra Nevada. 144 rooms.

Parador San Francisco (4 stars) €€€€ *Real de la Alhambra S/N; tel: 958 221 440; fax: 958 222 264.* Set within the precincts of the Alhambra, this historic *parador* is housed in the 15th-century Franciscan convent where Queen Isabella was originally interred. 46 rooms.

Hotel Carmen (4 stars) €€€ *Acera del Darro 62; tel: 958 258 300; fax: 958 256 462.* Modern hotel in the city centre close to the monuments. Full facilities, including restaurant, bar, pool and car park. 283 rooms.

Hotel Palacio de Santa Inés (3 stars) €€€€ *Cuesta de Santa Inés 9; tel: 958 222 362; fax: 958 222 465.* A 16th-century palace that has been beautifully converted into a hotel of considerable charm. Situated in the historic Albaicin area opposite to the towering Alhambra fortress. 6 rooms; 6 suites.

Maciá Gran Vía (3 stars) €€ *Gran Vía de Colón 25; tel: 958 285 464; fax: 958 285 591.* A very pleasant modern hotel conveniently located on the middle of the city's main street and just a few minutes' walk from the cathedral. Underground parking. 85 rooms.

Hotel Guadalupe (3 stars) €€ *Avenida los Alixares S/N; tel: 958 223 423; fax: 958 223 798.* Situated in the Alhambra complex very close to the monument, this is a comfortable hotel with a Granadino-style ambience. 58 rooms.

GUADIX

Hotel Comercio (2 stars) € *Avenida Mariana Pineda 65; tel: 958 661 500; fax: 958 660 179.* A short distance from the town centre and the intriguing Barrio Santiago. Recently modernised, it has very comfortable, large rooms and an excellent restaurant. 24 rooms.

GUILLENA

Hotel Cortijo Águila Real (4 stars) €€€ *Ctra. de Guillena–Burguillos, Km4; tel: 955 785 006; fax: 955 784 330.* A traditional ranch, just 24km (15 miles) from the centre of Sevilla. Beautifully converted rooms around the main yard, fine restaurant, inviting pool and a small bullring. 12 rooms.

JEREZ DE LA FRONTERA

Hotel Jerez (4 stars) €€€ *Avenida Alcalde Álvaro Domecq 35; tel: 956 300 600; fax: 956 305 001; <www.hoteljerez.com>.* Elegantly designed boutique hotel just a few minutes' walk away from all attractions. Large modern rooms, beautiful pool and gardens plus sports facilities. 126 rooms.

Hotel Guadalete (4 stars) €€€ *Avenida Duque de Abrantes 50; tel: 956 182 288; fax: 956 182 293.* Named after the famous battle, this exceptionally pleasant hotel is set in its own spacious grounds next to the Royal Equestrian school. It has an unusual mixture, but one that works well, of Southern Spanish and English decor. 125 rooms.

MÁLAGA

Hotel Larios (4 stars) €€€ *C/ Marques de Larios 2; tel: 952 222 200; fax: 952 222 407; <www.hotel-larios.com>.* Located in the main shopping centre by a pleasant square, the building dates from the beginning of the 20th century. It was completely renovated in 1999, and now has an art deco design and a dignified ambience. 40 rooms.

Hotel NH Málaga (4 stars) €€€ *Avenida Rio Guadalmedina s/n; tel: 952 071 323.* Opened in 1999, this hotel has a grand location just outside the old part of town. Impressive modern rooms, pleasant public areas and private parking. 133 rooms.

Parador Málaga-Gibralfaro (4 stars) €€€€ *Castillo de Gibralfaro S/N; tel: 952 221 902; fax: 952 221 904.* A small *parador*-grade hotel beside the Moorish castle on the hilltop above the city. Grand views over the city and the bay. 38 rooms.

Hotel Don Curro (3 stars) €€€ *C/ Sancha de Lara 7; tel: 952 227 200; fax: 952 215 946.* This is a long-established hotel with a very central location. All rooms have private baths and modern facilities. 120 rooms.

MARBELLA

Gran Meliá Don Pepe (5 stars) €€€€€ *José Meliá s/n; tel: 952 770 300; fax: 952 779 954; <www.solmelia.es>*. An imposing hotel just a 5-minute walk from the city centre. Only tropical gardens and pools separate it from the beach. Every expected luxury can be found here, plus a sports club with Jacuzzi and sauna and renowned restaurants. 202 rooms.

Don Carlos Beach & Golf Resort Hotel (5 stars) €€€€€ *Ctra de Cádiz, Km192; tel: 952 831 140; fax: 952 833 429; <www.hotel-doncarlos.com>*. Set in sub-tropical gardens on one of the best beaches on the coast. Totally renovated in the late 1990s with every possible luxury; views of Gibraltar and Africa; restaurants, bars, tennis and golf. 240 rooms.

Chapas Palacio del Sol (3 stars) €€€ *Ctra Cádiz, Km192; tel: 952 831 375; fax: 952 831 377*. Holiday complex set amid pine trees beside the beach about 8km (5 miles) east of town. Water sports facilities. 320 rooms.

EL PEURTO DE SANTA MARÍA

Hotel Monasterio San Miguel (4 stars) €€€€ *Calle Larga 27; tel: 956 540 440; fax: 956 542 604*. An intriguing complex originally constructed in the 18th century as a Capuchin convent. The cells and other rooms have been beautifully renovated in classical style to create an outstandingly interesting hotel. Previous guests include the Spanish royal family. 160 rooms.

RINCÓN DE LA VICTORIA

Hotel de Campo Molino de Santillana (2 stars) €€ *Ctra de Macharaviaya, Km3; tel: 952 115 780; fax: 952 215 782*. An attractive, small *cortijo*-style hotel east of Málaga in the Axarquía region. Set in its own grounds surrounded by almond, olive and fruit orchards, with vistas over the Mediterranean below. Fine restaurant. 10 rooms.

EL ROCÍO

Hotel Toruño (2 stars) €€ *Plaza del Acebuchal 22; tel: 959 442 323; fax: 959 442 338.* A delightful modern hotel in this historic and most unusual small town. It has views over the marshes of Doñana and the array of wildlife inhabiting it. 30 rooms.

RONDA

Hotel Reina Victoria (4 stars) €€€ *Dr. Fleming 25; tel: 952 871 240; fax: 952 871 075; email: <reinavictoriaronda@husa.es>*. Dating from 1906, but renovated to include all modern facilities, this hotel sits in its own attractive gardens and has panoramic views of the mountains. 90 rooms.

SEVILLA

Alfonso XIII (5 star GL) €€€€€ *San Fernando 2; tel: 954 222 850; fax: 954 216 033.* Opened by King Alfonso XIII in 1929, this imposing hotel in the city centre, set in its own lovely gardens, epitomises Sevillian style and luxury. Classically decorated, spacious rooms and a lobby bar that is a favourite meeting spot for Sevilla's high society. 149 rooms.

Hotel Taberna del Alabardero (4 stars) €€€€ *Zaragoza 20; tel: 954 560 637; fax: 954 563 666.* A Sevillian mansion converted into a small luxury hotel with exclusive, personalised service. The rooms, named not numbered, are set around a patio and combine modern facilities with the classy elegance of an earlier age. 10 rooms.

Hotel Los Seises (4 stars) €€€€ *Segovias 6; tel: 954 229 495; fax: 954 224 334.* An historic and beautiful 16th-century palace blending historic surroundings with modern facilities to create an intriguing ambience. Central location in Barrio de Santa Cruz. Rooftop pool overlooking the nearby cathedral and Giralda. 43 rooms.

Doña María (4 stars) €€€€ *Don Remonelo 19; tel: 954 224 940; fax: 954 219 546.* Agreeable hotel with an interesting mix of antiques and modern facilities. Excellent central location. A rooftop pool and bar are almost within touching distance of the Giralda and cathedral. 70 rooms.

Patios de Sevilla €€€€ *Patio de la Cartuja, Lumbreras 8–10; tel: 954 900 200; fax: 954 902 056* and **Patio de la Alameda**, *Alameda de Hercules 56; tel: 954 904 999; fax: 954 900 226*. Two typically Sevillan buildings, in a bohemian district, converted into modern apartments with a bedroom, sitting room with sofa bed, kitchen and bath. Private parking. 56 apartments.

Hotel Monte Triana (3 star) €€€ *Clara de Jesús Montero 24; tel: 954 343 111; fax: 954 343 328*. Found in the quieter Triana area, across the river and just 10 minutes' walk from the city centre. Nice atmosphere and large modern rooms and public areas. 117 rooms.

Hotel Simón (2 stars) €€ *García de Vinuesa 19; tel: 954 226 660; fax: 954 562 241*. Fine, handsome hotel set in a renovated 18th-century townhouse situated just across the street from the cathedral. 31 rooms.

TORREMOLINOS

Tropicana Hotel & Beach Club (4 stars) €€€ *Tropico 6, Box 29; tel: 952 386 600; fax: 952 380 568; <www.hotel-tropicana.net>*. Situated right on La Carihuela beach, this hotel has an interesting character and is set in its own small garden with a pool, beach club and prestigious Mango Restaurant. 85 rooms.

VILLANUEVA DE LA CONCEPCIÓN

La Posada del Torcal €€€ *Villanueva de la Concepción; tel: 952 031 177; fax: 952 031 006; email: <laposada@mercuryin.es>*. A small, luxurious Andalucían country *cortijo*. On an isolated hilltop, it has the rugged formations of El Torcal behind it and the Mediterranean shimmering in the far distance below. Pool, spa, sports facilities and gourmet restaurant. 10 rooms.

Recommended Restaurants

The establishments recommended here are mostly traditional Andalucían restaurants serving local specialities. The resorts along the coast are packed with cheaper (and blander) alternatives, ranging from fast-food outlets to Chinese, Indian and Italian restaurants.

Seafood restaurants line the waterfront in every town and are usually expensive – go inland for a block or two and the prices drop considerably, although the quality remains the same. Reservations are recommended for the more expensive places.

Lunch is generally served between 1.30 and 4pm and dinner between 9 and 11.30pm, although restaurants in the larger resorts tend to serve meals almost all day. As a basic guide to prices, we have used the following symbols to give some idea of the cost of lunch or dinner for two, not including drinks. All these restaurants accept the major credit cards unless otherwise noted.

€€€	over 60 euros
€€	36–60 euros
€	under 36 euros

BENALMÁDENA COSTA

Mar de Alborán €€ *Avenida de Alay 5; tel: 952 446 427.* Near the marina in Benalmádena, this Basque-Andalucían restaurant specialises in good, fresh seafood. Closed Sunday evening and all day Monday.

CARMONA

El Caballo Blanco €€€ *Plaza de Lasso 1; tel: 954 191 000.* The restaurant of the Casa de Carmona hotel, set in the wonderfully renovated stables of this former palace. The exquisite furniture, silverware and crystal complement the classically prepared international and Andalucían dishes. Altogether, a delightful experience.

CÓRDOBA

El Churrasco €€€ *Romero 16; tel: 957 290 817.* Seasonal cuisine and wines from their own Wine Museum, served in a 14th-century house in the Jewish Quarter. Closed August.

Almudaina €€€ *Camposanto de los Mártires 1; tel: 957 474 342.* A carefully restored 16th-century palace. Distinguished surroundings enhance the traditional Córdoban cuisine, prepared with fresh market produce. Closed Sunday night.

ESTEPONA

Lido Restaurant €€€ *Las Dunas Hotel, La Boladilla Baja, Ctra de Cádiz, Km163.5; tel: 952 796 554.* Supreme service, Mediterranean cuisine from a Michelin-starred chef, piano music and sea views.

FUENGIROLA

La Caracola €€ *Paseo Maritimo (Playa); tel: 952 584 687.* This restaurant on the beach has a relaxed ambience and serves specialities such as seafood casserole, small fried fish and fish baked in salt.

GRANADA

Chikito €€€ *Plaza del Campillo 9; tel: 958 223 364.* Typically Andalucían cuisine, a reasonably priced wine list and a city-centre location. Frequented by intellectuals and celebrities, whose photographs adorn the walls. Closed Wednesday.

Las Tinajas €€€ *Martínez Campos 17; tel: 958 254 393.* A popular meeting place, Las Tinajas specialises in local dishes. Vast international wine list. Closed July.

Sevilla €€ *Oficios 12; tel: 958 221 223.* Granada's most famous restaurant was once a favourite of the poet Federico García Lorca. The menu offers a good mix of local Granadino and Andalucían specialities. Closed Sunday evening.

JEREZ DE LA FRONTERA

El Bosque €€€ *Avenida Alcade Álvaro Domecq 26; tel: 956 312 020; fax: 956 308 008*. Prestigious restaurant serving traditional cuisine created with only the finest ingredients. Elegant dining rooms and a wine cellar of around 25,000 bottles. Closed Sunday.

Tendido 6 €€€ *Circo 10; tel: 956 344 835; fax: 956 330 374*. Next to the Plaza de Toros, with bull-themed decor to match. Wide menu of Andalucían cuisine and a mainly Spanish wine list.

EL MADROÑAL

Mesón El Coto €€€ *Ctra de Ronda (7km/4 miles from San Pedro); tel: 952 786 688; fax: 952 788 890*. In the foothills of the Serrania de Ronda mountains and overlooking the coast, this lovely restaurant specialises in rabbit, partridge, quail, duck, wild boar, baby lamb and suckling pig, which you cook yourself on a red-hot stone.

MÁLAGA

El Chinitas €€ *Moreno Monroy 4–6; tel: 952 210 972; fax: 952 220 031*. Restaurant in the Old Town, specialising in Andalucían and Málagueño dishes. Eat in or on the pedestrianised street in front.

Adolfo €€€ *Paseo Marítimo Pablo Ruiz Picasso 12; tel: 952 601 914*. Enjoy high-quality creative cooking with a menu that changes according to the season. Closed Sunday.

Bar Orellana € *Moreno Monroy 5; tel: 952 223 012*. No tables or chairs, just a small L-shaped bar and fabulous *tapas* that are popular with the locals, especially at weekends. Cash only.

Antigua Casa de Guardia € *Alameda Principal 18; tel: 952 214 680*. Founded in 1840 and hardly changed since. Huge wooden barrels of local wines, especially the sweet Málaga *dulce*, sit behind long wooden bars. Be sure to taste the small dishes of prawns, clams, mussels and other shellfish. Cash only.

MARBELLA

La Pesquera del Faro €€€ *Playa del Faro, Paseo Marítimo; tel: 952 868 520.* A pleasant restaurant in the Pesquera chain. This one, on the beach, does great seafood and has a wonderful ambience.

PUERTO DE BANUS

Taberna del Alabardero €€€ *Muelle Benabola S/N; tel: 952 812 794; fax: 952 818 630.* On the main quay overlooking the harbour, this prestigious restaurant offers Mediterranean and Basque specialities, as well as international selections.

EL PUERTO DE SANTA MARIA

El Faro del Puerto €€ *Ctra de Rota, Km0.5; tel: 956 858 003; fax: 956 540 466.* Surrounded by its own gardens, this restaurant is renowned for creative cuisine with traditional and imaginative dishes, and an extensive wine list. Closed Sunday night, except in August.

Romerijo €€€ *Plaza de la Herrería 1; tel: 956 541 254; fax: 956 541 006.* In a city famous for its seafood, this place, serving every variety of fish, is easily the most popular. Also does take-away.

SAN FERNANDO

Ventorrillo el Chato €€€ *Ctra de Cádiz a San Fernando, Km687; tel: 956 250 225; fax: 956 253 222.* On the isthmus connecting Cádiz to San Fernando, this is a historic restaurant with an attractive Andalucían-style dining room. It has Andalucían-style cuisine, too, with tasty desserts and fine wines. Closed Sunday.

SEVILLA

Casa Robles €€ *Alvarez Quintero 58; tel: 954 563 272.* This restaurant, in an 18th-century mansion very close to the cathedral, is popular with locals and tourists alike. Does traditional Andalucían stews and seafood dishes along with home-made desserts.

Egaña Oriza €€€ *San Fernando 41; tel: 954 427 211; fax: 954 502 727.* Located in a beautiful building opposite the tobacco factory, Egaña Oriza is renowned for dishes that combine Basque influences with Andalucían traditions. Spanish and international wine list. Closed Saturday lunchtime, Sunday and August.

Mesón Don Raímundo €€ *Argote de Molina 26; tel: 954 223 355; fax: 954 218 951.* Housed in a former 14th-century convent, this place does a fully Andalucían menu, with excellent game and delicious desserts.

Horacio € *Antonio Díaz 9; tel: 954 225 385.* Situated close to the Plaza de Toros, the appealing Horacio has a creatively modern ambience, with Andalucían and international cuisine to match.

Los Seises €€€ *Segovias 6; tel: 954 229 495.* In the hotel of the same name, this restaurant, set around Roman and Moorish excavations, offers top regional cuisine and desserts with Arabic influences.

La Albahaca €€€ *Plaza Santa Cruz 12; tel: 954 220 714; fax: 954 561 204.* Housed in a typical Sevillian mansion, La Albahaca offers three dining rooms and alfresco dining in summer. Basque-based menu with exquisite seasonal dishes. Closed Sunday.

Corral del Agua €€€ *Agua 6; tel: 954 224 851; fax: 954 561 204.* An attractive 17th-century house in the Barrio de Santa Cruz. Classic Andalucían cuisine. Lovely patio around a fountain. Closed Sunday.

El Rinconcillo € *Gerona 40–42; tel: 954 223 183.* One of the oldest and most atmospheric *tapas* bars in the city, dating from the 17th century. A running account of your bill is chalked up on the wall.

TORREMOLINOS

La Langosta €€ *Bulto 53; tel: 952 384 381; fax: 952 370 498.* On the Paseo Marítimo on the famous La Carihuela beach in the fishermen's quarter. Marine atmosphere, seafood specialities, wines from Spain, Germany and France and a menu in 10 languages.

INDEX